WEEKNIGHT
PALEO

WEEKNIGHT PALEO

100+ EASY AND DELICIOUS FAMILY-FRIENDLY MEALS

Julie and Charles Mayfield

WILLIAM MORROW

An Imprint of HarperCollins*Publishers*

ALSO BY JULIE AND CHARLES MAYFIELD

Paleo Comfort Foods
Quick & Easy Paleo Comfort Foods

HarperCollins books may be purchased for educational, business, or sales promotional use. For information please e-mail the Special Markets Department at SPsales@harpercollins.com.

FIRST EDITION

Designed by Suet Yee Chong
Photography © Mark Adams

Library of Congress Cataloging-in-Publication Data has been applied for.

ISBN 978-0-06-241965-1

17 18 19 20 21   ID/QDG   1 2 3 4 5 6 7 8 9 10

To Scott and Adelyn,
who make all our days the "best day ever"

CONTENTS

Introduction ix

What Is Paleo? 1

Family Favorites 24

Fix and Forget 70

Get Your Veggies 88

One-Dish Meals 108

Quickfire Meals 140

Sauces and Staples 206

Sweets and Treats 230

Acknowledgments........................... 247
Resources.................................. 249
Universal Conversion Chart 251
Index 253

INTRODUCTION

Let's face it: We live in a fast-paced world, and many of us find ourselves with jam-packed schedules—shuttling kids or pets or ourselves to and from this or that, commuting, evening work commitments, trying to make time for our significant others, friends, family, church . . . indeed our lives are a pretty far cry from our ancestors' way of living in all that we do. We no longer live in villages where all of our friends, family members, and necessities are literally a stone's throw away, where our jobs keep us outdoors pretty much every day, where walking and socializing (in person) and sharing meals are all a part of our daily lives. Our modern lifestyle presents some serious challenges as it relates to keeping us and our families out of the drive-thru and in the kitchen. This book will show that it is possible to make nourishing, satisfying, and delicious meals and not lose your life to grocery shopping and cooking.

One of the biggest challenges we hear that people face is finding or making time to cook meals. While one could argue it's a matter of priorities (it's reported that the average American spends nearly three hours per day watching TV and about half an hour per day on food preparation and cleanup), we know for many houses that is certainly not the case, and finding time to cook from scratch can be extremely difficult. Sometimes, it just takes getting a little creative, or a little planning ahead, or a new technique (like not thawing out the steak before cooking it!—see the recipe on page 197) to help make dinnertime at home possible.

Our goal in writing this book is to provide real recipes for real families who want to feed everyone nutritious, delicious meals—without spending too much of their lives in the kitchen. We aren't saying that you don't need to do any planning or any work; there will be some slicing and dicing. We are saying that there are ways to make getting dinner on the table a little less stressful—heck, maybe even fun for you (and the kids if they're in the picture). In this book you'll find recipes that we make a lot in our house, and dozens of ideas on how to make eating nutritious food at home possible without eating the same thing twenty-one meals in a row.

We're fortunate in that we did not come to a Paleo lifestyle by way of some autoimmune disease, some adverse health issues, or with a ton of weight we needed to lose. However, we both have years of experience with scale fluctuations, experimenting with what we choose to eat and when, in addition to a variety of athletic pursuits. When it comes to "diets," we've tried NutriSystem, SlimFast, the Zone Diet, the 6 Week Body Makeover, vegetarianism, a bunch of programs touted by celebrities, the cabbage soup diet, cleanses, and many others. While we weren't yo-yo dieters, we both have had many ups and downs with the scale.

We first heard of "Paleo" as it related to a way of eating in 2008. We had recently started dating and were heavily smitten with each other . . . and with CrossFit workouts. Like many in the CrossFit world, we're ever thankful it provided us with our introduction to each other, to Paleo, and to Robb Wolf. We attended Robb's CrossFit certification—the "Paleolithic Solution Seminar"—in 2009, where Robb finally got Charles to stop meticulously (obsessively?) counting almonds. For us, the Paleo way of eating made perfect sense. Here was something that had helped so many people look, feel, and perform better and was so squarely focused on eating real foods and omitting the processed junk that lines the grocery store aisles. We were sold. Many other diets and lifestyle plans were either trying to sell you something (their branded products) to make certain "pseudo-foods" a mainstay of a diet or just plain did not make sense as to what would or could promote great health. A breakfast composed of eggs, sautéed vegetables, and some avocado? A lunch of a huge bowl of pasture-raised chicken and vegetable soup? A dinner of grilled grass-fed steak, sautéed Brussels sprouts, and mashed sweet potato? What wasn't to love?

Then in 2010, over a NorCal margarita or several, Robb and his wife, Nicki Violetti, suggested that we write a cookbook featuring some of the recipes we'd been enjoying at home. A year later, our first book—*Paleo Comfort Foods*—was released, followed by *Quick & Easy Paleo Comfort*

Foods about two years later. At the same time, we started growing our family. Our pattern was birth a book, birth a baby, birth a book, birth a baby. We're pretty certain that after this book there will not be more babies, but we do hope to continue writing books!

While a basic Paleo template might work wonders for some, we're not going to say that it's perfect for everyone. We will stand by our belief that sourcing things responsibly, eating real, nutrient-dense foods, eliminating or at least greatly reducing the amount of food we eat that has added (refined) sugars or comes from a package, eating home-cooked meals, and sharing meals with family or friends are core principles that seem to make a whole bunch of sense.

At the end of the day, we are not here to preach; rather, we want you to know that we are in your corner, in your shoes, and we know that sometimes we are going to call in the reinforcements by way of a Paleo meal delivery service or hitting up Chipotle. That's not the end of our world, nor should it be for you. However, for the majority of the time, we hope that the recipes and resources in this book help make home-cooked meals the norm for you, rather than the exception. It's what you all deserve!

Happy cooking!
Julie and Charles
(and the wee ones!)

WHAT IS PALEO?

A quick Google search of "what is Paleo" yields more than twenty million results. You'll find websites that talk about this way of eating with images of a Fred Flintstone–like caricature gnawing on a huge piece of meat. You'll find some stating it's a low-carb, high-protein diet. If you venture into any of the thousands of CrossFit gyms around the world and ask someone to define Paleo, you're likely to get just as many different answers, with maybe even a few people chowing down on a big piece of meat just like Mr. Flintstone.

While you will have some very dogmatic folks insisting that there is only one true Paleo diet, we tend to disagree. Just like we think that our ancestors 200,000 years ago didn't all eat the exact same things as one another in the exact same amounts and macronutrient profiles, we like to think the same concepts apply to all of us. Where you live, your activity level, your personal preference, what you have access to, and your unique needs can and should play a big role in determining what you eat. In our opinion, and seemingly more and more the opinion of some leaders in the ancestral health community (like Chris Kresser, Robb Wolf, Mark Sisson, and others), it is far more appropriate to think of Paleo as a template as opposed to a diet with hard and fast rules. Diets that work for some might not, and usually do not, work for all; and Paleo in a strict sense is no exception.

While some folks think that Paleo is strictly "eating the way our ancestors ate," we aren't huge fans of that definition. For starters, in today's world, there is almost no possible way to eat just like our ancestors ate, work like they worked, or sleep like they slept. For example, many of the foods they ate aren't even close to being available in today's world. The tubers and berries they likely would have eaten and the types of animals they would have hunted are not much like the Garnet sweet potatoes, strawberries, and grass-fed beef we now have access to.

That said, there are some core tenets of what our ancestors did or did not eat that make sense to us:

- They ate real, nutrient-dense foods that came from plants, shrubs, trees, and other living creatures. End of story. They didn't have manufactured foods.

- They ate a wide variety of foods. We're pretty sure a caveman would have been ousted from the community or would have died of hunger if he or she ate only boneless, skinless chicken breasts. Indeed, our ancestors likely ate from nose-to-tail of every living creature, something that is definitely not the norm in our culture.

- Some days they ate a lot, some days, not so much.

- They ate seasonally and locally available foods. They weren't traipsing across the globe for weeks on end to get their hands on tomatoes grown thousands of miles away and bringing them back to their homes in the dead of winter.

- Their sugar consumption was limited to real sugars occurring in real foods.

- They didn't eat things that came in a package or a box, with a long list of artificial ingredients.

- They typically ate as part of a community, sharing meals with their tribe.

Most of these principles aren't so impossible to incorporate into our own day-to-day lives, but they can seem overwhelming to some.

Everywhere we turn we are bombarded by seemingly conflicting messages as to what will make us our healthiest selves yet, what foods are best for us, and how to go about losing those last ten pounds. This is exactly why over half of Americans polled in a 2012 report stated that they believe it's easier to figure out their income taxes than to figure out what they should and shouldn't eat to be healthier.* Now that's some scary stuff!

OUR PALEO DEFINITION

Our personal Paleo prescription (that we apply at home) is this: We eat meat, seafood, vegetables, fruits, nuts, and fats. We prioritize our protein choices to be mostly those from grass-fed, pasture-raised, wild-caught origins. We strive to make our plates or bowls half full of vegetables, include fats at all our meals, and try to eat as seasonally and locally as possible. We'll use dairy in the form of grass-fed butter and some heavy cream; and sometimes we might splurge for an ice cream treat. As food writer Michael Ruhlman wrote in the *Washington Post,* "Our food is not healthy; we will be healthy if we eat nutritious food." Our Paleo prescription reflects that sentiment—we eat nutritious foods that make us feel healthy.

When people ask us what our Paleo template is like, we typically steer clear of dogma, and instead speak about what we in our little family eat. We usually describe the foods we *do* eat first, rather than talking about what we don't eat. For example, we might say, "Oh, yesterday through the course of the day I ate broccoli, cauliflower, zucchini, squash, sauerkraut, a kale salad, sweet potato, some grilled chicken, scrambled eggs, bacon, and some pork tenderloin. Oh, and some avocado, olive oil, and grass-fed butter. (Sadly, the fact that vegetables are a mainstay of this way of eating often gets overlooked and overshadowed by this caveman persona, despite the fact that for most in the Paleo world this is not a high-protein diet.) We find that telling people about all the "yes!" foods is a lot more helpful than starting out with the nos.

Turn the page for a handy chart for Paleo beginners.

* International Food Information Council Foundation 2012 Food and Health Survey

EAT THESE	AVOID THESE (AT LEAST TO START OUT)
Red meat, game, pork, fish, seafood, eggs, poultry	Grains
Vegetables of all varieties	Legumes
Fruits	Dairy
Nuts and Seeds	Processed foods
Spices and Herbs	Sugars
Healthy fats (olive oil, coconut oil, tallow, lard, etc.)	Alcohol

Grains: While some anthropologists are splitting hairs over whether or not hunter-gatherers ate certain things (like grains), we'll never really know for certain what our ancestors ate, and to us it really does not matter. What we do know about modern-day grains is this: They aren't essential for our day-to-day, healthiest lives. For some people (like those with celiac disease), gluten-containing grains can be a hospital admission. For most people, there is little nutritional benefit to grains that cannot be gained from fruits and vegetables. Fiber? It's great! And you can get lots of fiber from all the vegetables and fruits you should be eating. Vitamins and minerals? Calorie for calorie, veggies and fruits will give you much more than grains. Grains will give you lots of empty calories—especially most of the refined, processed grain food products you find out there. Grains have some potentially problematic antinutrients (lectins, gluten, and phytates) that don't do many favors for a lot of people. You might be one of them. Try completely removing grains for thirty days and see how you feel, then maybe experiment with adding back things like white rice to see how you do.

Legumes: Legumes (which include beans, peas, lentils, and peanuts) are what many vegans and vegetarians cite as a perfect protein source. While legumes do contain protein, they do not contain nutrients we cannot get elsewhere and they aren't as nutrient-dense as other foods. Whether or not Neanderthals ate beans is irrelevant, in our opinion. What is important is that if you take legumes out of your diet for a period of time, then reintroduce them (and prepare them properly), there's no reason that they might not be included in your Paleo template if you tolerate them well.

Dairy: Dairy is a pretty polarizing topic in Paleo circles. Some claim that we're the only species that drinks another animal's breast milk, and that there's a reason we as humans wean at a certain age. On the flip side, we once heard someone ponder whether we were the smarter species because we figured out how to milk another creature. All that aside, there are people who simply do not tolerate dairy well at all. We happen to do okay on dairy, so we tend to include the occasional piece of cheese, some grass-fed butter, and some grass-fed heavy cream in our lives—and maybe ice cream every once in a while! Note: We do give some dairy-based options or alterations in this book, and we prefer grass-fed dairy in these instances.

Processed foods/sugars/alcohol: Processed foods, sugars, and alcohol can all be delicious. But if you are going to argue that they are making you healthier, we beg to differ. And by processed foods we aren't talking about the basic processing it took to get that grass-fed cow into your freezer, or the processing it took to get that olive oil into a bottle. We're talking about things in a package or a box at the store with all kinds of ingredients that are manufactured. We're talking about those snack crackers, candies, and breads that might have claims on the label of being "enriched" or "fortified" or "kid-tested, mother-approved" that most likely aren't moving us toward our healthiest selves. Sugar and alcohol also go here. We aren't claiming that we never have anything from a package, never consume sugar, or never enjoy a glass of wine or cider. Rather, for those first starting out with Paleo, the best way to see how you react to certain foods and beverages is to eliminate them for a period of time.

After trying a pretty clean way of Paleo eating, then we suggest slowly starting to add things back in and see how you feel. Does dairy make your skin break out? Do grains make you bloated? Does sugar give you headaches? Take your personal experience into consideration. Just like some people think certain perfumes and colognes smell great while others need to clear the room to avoid the smell, so, too, do individuals have unique reactions to food. We are not all the same in our reactions and such things need to be noted.

We would be remiss if we didn't discuss "cheating." For starters, we don't like to think of our decisions to eat not-very-nutritious food as "cheating." Rather, if we choose to have something that is decidedly "not Paleo," or has added sugar, or isn't moving us to be healthier, it's merely a choice we made, and we don't deem it "cheating." The word "cheating" revolves around dishonesty and deceit, so as long as you're being honest with yourself about the choice you're making, as long as you're mindful about choosing to have some of those candy-coated chocolates, then we don't think you're "cheating"—rather, you are opting for something that you've decided is worth having. Then again, we view this way of eating as just how we live—we do not view this as a temporary diet after which we go back to eating junk food throughout our days. Even if we choose to eat a doughnut or big loaf of bread, we don't demonize those choices for ourselves or for anyone else. We know if we make such choices how they will make us feel (usually lousy, lethargic, and bloated). We believe that no food is inherently healthy, but some foods are more nutritious than others, and we choose to include more of the nutritious stuff in our lives than the non-nutritive stuff.

TRANSITIONING TO PALEO

While some people are "all or nothing" as it relates to habits, others need to take baby steps when transitioning (Gretchen Rubin's book *Better Than Before* and website gretchenrubin.com offer great insight on habit formation), it really depends on how you are wired, and before embarking on any health journey we encourage you to do a little introspection to figure out more about yourself (the aforementioned book and website do wonders to help with that). It makes no sense to try to establish some new habit if it goes completely against your lifestyle (hitting the gym at five a.m. for someone who is a night owl might be a recipe for disaster). Whether you use the recipes in this book once in a while to help transition the family slowly but surely, or you go whole hog and plan a month's worth of meals, we are here to support you. Part of figuring out how to successfully transition to any new way of eating or living is figuring out a bit about yourself, so invest that time and energy to help you become as successful as possible! The resource section found on pages 249–50 provides a listing of our favorite sources of information, but some of our favorite Paleo resources to get you started include:

- Robb Wolf's Quick Start Guide: Robbwolf.com

- Chris Kresser's *The Paleo Cure*: Chriskresser.com

- Melissa Hartwig's *The Whole30*: Whole30.com

PUTTING IT ALL TOGETHER
HOW THE HECK DO YOU FEED A BUSY, BUDGET-CONSCIOUS FAMILY?

Now that we have kids along with our businesses, sometimes life can be a bit unpredictable (like when a child needs to go to the emergency room for stitches) and stressful (like when a pig gets out of the fencing), and sometimes ordering a gluten-free pizza seems like the easy solution. However, we know that our two little kiddos depend on us for their nutrients. We aren't saying we never opt for a gluten-free pizza, but of the roughly ninety or so meals in a given month, we guess that less than five of those meals are eaten at a restaurant or are takeout. Not only does this enable us to focus on healthy foods for us and our kids, but it also helps keep our budget in check.

We will be the first to admit that sometimes getting dinner on the table is a challenge in and of itself, yet there is lots of research showing why we should all try to make the family meal a priority. For starters, fewer calories are typically consumed at home as opposed to eating out.[*] There is research indicating that children and teens who eat more meals at home are less likely to become overweight or obese,[†] and that teens

---

[*] R. An (2015). "Fast-Food and Full-Service Restaurant Consumption and Daily Energy and Nutrient Intakes in US Adults." *European Journal of Clinical Nutrition* doi: 10.1038/ejcn.2015.104. www.ncbi.nlm.nih.gov/pubmed/26130301

[†] AJ. Hammons (2011). "Is Frequency of Shared Family Meals Related to the Nutritional Health of Children and Adolescents?" *Pediatrics*, 127;e1565; pediatrics.aappublications.org/content/127/6/e1565.

who eat family meals together frequently are less likely to use drugs and alcohol or smoke tobacco. Those are some pretty decent reasons to at least consider eating as a family. As we are admittedly about the opposite of Type A people, you won't come to our house and see every single meal for the week pristinely mapped out with our ingredients ordered in the refrigerator alphabetically or by date of anticipated use. Rather, we usually have a discussion about what we think sounds good that particular week, often letting our cooking be guided by what is fresh and available at our weekly farmers' market (we will talk more about sourcing your ingredients on page 14) and more often than not we're looking in our freezer and taking out a few pounds of various meats over the weekend, and placing them in a bowl in the refrigerator to thaw out for a few days. We often will do a lot of cooking on a Sunday to get us through the first few days of the week, and if we're firing up the grill you'll almost never see just one serving of something on it!

MEAL PLANNING

Love it or loathe it, it's pretty well established that meal planning can help save you money, time, and perhaps your sanity when it comes to getting dinner on the table. So, even though some of these recipes are prepped and on the table in under thirty minutes, that doesn't help if you have to trek twenty minutes to the grocery store every night to pick up ingredients you're missing. Meal planning is definitely one of the keys to success in helping families eat healthier foods at home.

Here are our suggestions for successful meal planning:

- Get some kind of calendar or organizer, use a white board, or anything that provides a place for you to write down your plans. There are lots of free downloadable meal planning templates and fancy notebook planners available to help with this process. You can also download ours for free on our website paleocomfortfoods.com (or make copies of the meal planning template on page 13).

- Schedule time to plan and put it on your calendar. There's a saying: "What gets scheduled gets done." That doctor's appointment, that lunch date with a friend—once those things get scheduled, they get done (for the most part). The same is true for meal planning. If you put on your calendar a dedicated thirty minutes to plan, then you're more likely to get it done.

- Assess your household and your week ahead. Do your kids get lunch at school? Do you have plans to go out to dinner on Friday night? Do you have a three-day conference when you'll be gone and away from home? Do your kids have soccer until seven p.m. and you need dinner on the table right after? These should all factor into your assessment of the week.

- Decide what is realistic for your household. If you currently eat dinner out several times a week, making the jump to saying "no eating out" could be a bit too extreme. Decide what

is going to be realistic, perhaps starting with "We'll have dinner at home four times this week."

- Think about what is in season and use that to inform some of your planning. (See the list on page 19 for general guidelines on what is in season when.) If you do much of your shopping at your local farmers' market, sometimes it can feel overwhelming to see so many vegetables and fruits. It can be helpful to have some sense of a game plan ahead of time to help direct your shopping exploits.

- Figure out what you already have on hand, as well as what you're running low on. This does two things: First, it helps you make use of what you have available. Second, it helps keep your pantry, refrigerator, or freezer stocked with staples. For example, when we have a freezer full of beef or pork cuts (like when we participate in a cow or pig share), many of our recipes for the upcoming week will likely focus more on those cuts than chicken or fish. Often we take stock of what staples, veggies, and fats we have on hand and see what recipes spring to mind. Another tip from our house: We like to keep a running list on a notepad or whiteboard of the things we are running low on. That way, if we don't have much chicken stock on hand, we can plan to make some (page 209) or buy some more.

- Especially for the budget-conscious: Make your list and stick to it. How many of you have gone shopping at Target or Costco or Whole Foods for something specific and somehow ended up spending way more money than you planned on? Make that list and stick to it. If you really want to up your budgeting, follow Dave Ramsey's envelope method—that is, set aside an envelope with the budgeted amount of cash for your groceries that week (or month).

- Keep a list of your favorite or itching-to-try recipes somewhere (on Pinterest, in Evernote, or in a favorite notebook). Keep track of where to find them if they are not hyperlinked (e.g., if you're using a notebook, write "Page [xxx] of *Weeknight Paleo*"). Make sure, once you've made certain recipes, to write down what you loved about them or any alterations you made. For example, "Used chicken instead of beef. Loved it." "Kids devoured this. Will double it next time."

Here's a sample approach:
1. On the calendar, identify what nights it will be realistic to devote thirty minutes to one hour to cooking. We note those with a "C."
2. If you know there will be meals away from home, note those. We simply write "Out."
3. For nights when you need dinner on the table in five to ten minutes after you all come in the door, set up a slow cooker meal earlier in the day or have leftovers at the ready. We put an "F" on those days, meaning "Fast."

A typical week for us might indicate that we have three nights we'll have time to cook dinner, three nights when we need leftovers or a slow cooker meal, and one night out. Now that we have that information, we can populate our calendar with what meals we plan on cooking or eating and when. Here's a sample week with recipes from this book.

SUNDAY	MONDAY	TUESDAY	WEDNESDAY	THURSDAY	FRIDAY	SATURDAY
C	F	C	F	C	F	Out
Double batch Basic Roast Chicken (page 26), with Broccoli Salad (page 92)	Use leftover chicken for Chinois Chicken Salad (page 150)	One-Pan-Fajitas (page 120) with Lime Chipotle Slaw (page 94)	Carnitas (slow cooker—page 73) with leftover chipotle slaw from Tuesday	Double batch Italian Meatballs (page 52), with 5-Ingredient Tomato Sauce (page 214) over zucchini noodles	Italian meatball leftovers	

This is just a sample, but as you can see it keeps you from being a slave to your kitchen. We almost always make sure to double or triple our recipes, as we eat leftovers for breakfasts or lunches most of the time. (You can easily add in a lunch row to your calendar to add those meals in for planning purposes.) Any leftovers beyond what we know we can consume in a few days can usually be frozen so we have our "emergency—thaw and reheat" foods on hand.

Most people find it easiest to do their planning and grocery shopping on the weekends because that's when they have some time to do so. (Many local farmers' markets are on Saturdays, so we can vouch for that being a good idea.) Do what works for you.

YOU'VE MADE YOUR PLAN, NOW WHAT?

Now you're ready to get ready—if that makes sense! Meaning, you've made your plan, and now you need to:

1. Create your shopping lists (taking into account what you have on hand) and hit your market(s). There's a great website called Pepperplate where you can input your favorite recipes and create shopping lists based on the recipes you've selected. (The downside is that you have to input the recipes, but once you've done that, it's a great timesaver.)
2. If you have older kids, have them help you with the shopping as that is less work for you and more fun for them than being dragged along to the grocery store with nothing to do!
3. When you come home from your shopping, schedule a time as soon as possible to organize your goods. If you'll be cooking something that day, set out the nonperishable ingredients you know you'll need straight away. We like to use a baking sheet to lay out the ingredients for a given recipe—plus that helps us see if we are missing anything.
4. If you have some extra time, seize the opportunity to do just a little bit more to get ahead of the game. If you are making something that calls for a commonly used ingredient (like diced or sliced onions, peppers, or minced garlic) and you know you'll be using that same ingredient within the next few

WEEKLY MENU PLAN

MONDAY

TUESDAY

WEDNESDAY

THURSDAY

FRIDAY

SATURDAY

SUNDAY

GROCERY SHOPPING LIST

STAPLES

HOUSEHOLD

PRODUCE

MEAT/SEAFOOD

REFRIGERATED

FROZEN

HEALTH/BEAUTY

MISCELLANEOUS

days, prep some extra and place it in a resealable bag or small container for future use. If you know you're making fajitas tomorrow, slice the meat ahead of time so that part of the prep is already done.

5. Check your plan against what you will need during the week (aside from what you just shopped for). Going to need beef later in the week? Now is a great time to take it out of the freezer, place it in a bowl in the refrigerator, and let it thaw over the next two days or so.

FOOD SOURCING AND SUSTAINABILITY

To be interested in food but not in food production is clearly absurd.

—Wendell Berry

The food we eat is as far from nature as our lifestyle. We consume animals that were raised in factories and vegetables that were sprayed with chemicals and harvested by people who can't afford to eat what they pick.

—Diana Rodgers, *The Homegrown Paleo Cookbook*

We're big proponents of doing the best you can with what you have. Trying to tell everyone reading this book that they should grow their own food all year round is not the message we are trying to convey. Rather, it's important—essential even—that anyone as a consumer understands what they are purchasing and how that food came into being. Not from a "how did I get here?" philosophical standpoint, but rather "what were the conditions for that animal's life? How are the farmworkers who helped harvest those vegetables treated? How did that chocolate come into being in your hand?"

There's no one clear, right definition of the word "sustainable" as it relates to food production, but we like what the Sustainable Food Lab states: "We define a sustainable food and agriculture system as one in which the fertility of our soil is maintained and improved; the availability and quality of water are protected and enhanced; our biodiversity is protected; farmers, farm workers, and all other actors in value chains have livable incomes; the food we eat is affordable and promotes our health; sustainable businesses can thrive; and the flow of energy and the discharge of waste, including greenhouse gas emissions, are within the capacity of the earth to absorb forever." Essentially, sustainable food is real food that is good for us, good for the environment, good for the people growing and harvesting it, and is humane for the animals and people caring for them. Sounds pretty good to us!

Let's think about that for a moment. Take, for example, the notion of wanting sustainable food to be good for the people growing and harvesting it. Did you know that child slavery is very much a real issue in other parts of the world, and that the very chocolate bar you love might

be in your hands because of child slaves? As parents, we shudder to think of the terrible treatment some children endured just to put that candy bar in someone's Easter basket, and yet that is a very real issue. What can you do? For starters, don't buy chocolates that come from non–fair trade sources. (Diana Rodgers has a great discussion of this in *The Homegrown Paleo Cookbook* and on her website, sustainabledish.com.)

What about being good for the environment? Is that really important? In a nutshell, more than you can possibly imagine. Did you know that some 40 percent of soil used for agriculture around the world is classified as either degraded or seriously degraded, and it's estimated that if our world keeps running like it is, we have only about sixty years of topsoil left? What does that mean? For starters, soil is imperative for water retention, and degraded soil cannot hold water as well as healthy soil. Also, degraded soil means less productive soil. You cannot feed growing populations with less food, and it's estimated that degraded soil will produce 30 percent less food over the next twenty to fifty years. This is some scary stuff!

So what can you as an individual do? Sometimes it all feels overwhelming, like there is so much to do that you almost feel paralyzed and unable to do anything. As we've stated before, do what you can, even if it's something that seems small or insignificant. We think this quote sums up this notion nicely:

I am only one,
But still I am one.
I cannot do everything,
But still I can do something;
And because I cannot do everything,
I will not refuse to do the something that I can do.

—Edward Everett Hale

If we all took just one tiny step toward doing something to make change, collectively that makes for a much bigger step. Here are a few of our suggestions for living a bit more sustainably:

- Shop at your local farmers' market. Your food dollars are your ballots, and every time you shop at a local farmers' market you're casting a vote for a more sustainable system. Support them year-round if possible. Don't have the budget for a farmers' market? See if any of your local farms offer bartering. Perhaps you're a fabulous Web designer just starting out, and the local farm needs a new website. If your work can benefit them, you might be able to get some great items in exchange for your services. Be creative.

- Eat locally and seasonally as much as possible, and preserve what you can. Freezing that bumper crop of blueberries and canning those homegrown tomatoes are a great way to live sustainably year-round.

- Grow whatever you can! If you don't have the space, see if there's a local community garden you can join. Or try planting some windowsill herbs like basil and rosemary. Even such seemingly small steps make a difference.

- If you are purchasing from a larger retailer, look for labels that indicate how your food came into being. For example, animal welfare approved, fair trade, certified organic, certified humane, certified Paleo, and Paleo approved all give you as the consumer some insights into the vetting process for that particular item.

> *You, as a food buyer, have the distinct privilege*
> *of proactively participating in shaping*
> *the world your children will inherit.*
>
> —Joel Salatin, *Holy Cows and Hog Heaven: The*
> *Food Buyer's Guide to Farm Friendly Food*

In a perfect world, we'd have a food system that was unbridled to evolve and transform to the needs of its community. According to the Center for Urban Education about Sustainable Agriculture (CUESA), the average American meal travels some fifteen hundred miles from farm to plate. As best we can, we need to get back to our local roots, our local farms, our local agriculture. While it's great that we can have any food flown in or shipped in from anywhere across the globe, is that sustainable and responsible on a day-to-day basis?

A bonus to all this is that indeed, things like shopping locally and in season can help bring your food costs down. Of course, growing things yourself also makes most of these items far less expensive. But even if you don't have a green thumb, buying what is in season at the grocery store can still save you a decent amount of money, because when crops are at their most widely available, there's a lot of supply and the prices are usually lower. Fortunately, most farmers' markets are only going to offer what's in season (your local growers won't be selling heirloom tomatoes in the dead of winter), so that can help you determine what's in season.

While the list on the opposite page does not include everything, it can give you a sense of what might be in season and when (generally speaking, as this relates to North America). That's not to say that you should never buy garlic out of season, or that cauliflower should be eaten only in fall or winter. Rather, if you're looking for locally sourced produce, or when things might be on sale, this might help.

WHAT YOU'LL FIND IN THIS BOOK

The recipes you'll find here are those that we cook at home, and as such, they represent what we eat. For example, we don't have twenty desserts here because we don't make desserts at home that often. Why? Because we know we have a weakness for sugar (whether honey or coconut sugar or refined sugar—sugar is sugar is sugar), and too much sugar (even Paleo-oriented baked goods) doesn't help us feel our best. We also don't include a lot of offal recipes. Though we try to include offal in our diet when we think about it, it's not on our favorites list, and quite honestly, usually takes a good amount of time to prepare. We do mention liver with our All-American Burgers (page 41), and if you can sneak some in there, do it! All that is to say that we wanted this book to be an accurate representation of our lives and what recipes are in our regular rotation.

WHAT'S IN SEASON WHEN

WINTER (DECEMBER–FEBRUARY)	SPRING (MARCH–MAY)	SUMMER (JUNE–AUGUST)	FALL (SEPTEMBER–NOVEMBER)	YEAR-ROUND
Acorn squash	Artichokes	Apricots	Apples	Avocado
Apples	Arugula	Blackberries	Broccoli	Bananas
Brussels sprouts	Asparagus	Blueberries	Broccoli rabe	Bok choy
Butternut squash	Bibb lettuce	Boysenberries	Brussels sprouts	Broccoli
Cauliflower	Cauliflower	Broccoli	Cabbage	Celery
Clementines	Chard	Cantaloupe	Cauliflower	Lemons
Collard greens	Fennel	Cherries	Cranberries	Limes
Grapefruit	Garlic	Cherry tomatoes	Fennel	Mushrooms
Kale	Green beans	Corn	Garlic	Onions
Kiwi fruit	Peas	Cucumbers	Grapes	Spinach
Oranges	Radicchio	Currants	Kale	
Pears	Radishes	Eggplant	Kohlrabi	
Pomegranates	Rhubarb	Endive	Leeks	
Potatoes	Salad greens	Figs	Pears	
Root vegetables	Spinach	Grapes	Peppers	
Sweet potatoes	Strawberries	Green beans	Pomegranates	
Tangerines	Vidalia onions	Green peppers	Potatoes	
Winter squash		Honeydew	Pumpkin	
		Hot peppers	Quince	
		Kale	Root vegetables	
		Nectarine	Salad Greens	
		Okra		
		Peaches		
		Peas		
		Plums		
		Radishes		
		Raspberries		
		Salad Greens		
		Summer squash		
		Tomatillos		
		Tomatoes		
		Turnips		
		Watermelon		
		Zucchini		

INGREDIENTS

We hope that you will strive for using the best ingredients you can, whether it's a matter of access or budget. These are our preferences when we include the following ingredients in a recipe:

- **Almond flour:** finely ground, blanched almond flour
- **Beef:** grass-fed and grass-finished
- **Chicken:** pasture-raised
- **Chocolate:** fair trade, organic
- **Coconut milk:** full-fat without sugar added
- **Coconut oil:** fair trade, organic
- **Pork:** pasture-raised
- **Salt:** kosher salt or fine sea salt

If you can source locally—even better! If not, do the best you can. If you are unable to get grass-fed beef for whatever reason, we'd rather see you do the best you can with the meat you can get instead of falling face first into some macaroni and cheese from a box! Organic is great too, but some of our favorite farms we've visited are not certified organic, so we don't get spun up on the organic labeling. If you know your farmers and their practices, that really helps in informing you as the consumer. Some farms with some of the best, cleanest practices are not certified organic, like the well-known Polyface Farms in Swoope, Virginia. However, their practices are in fact "beyond organic"; they just haven't gone through the paperwork and administrative detail required to become certified through the US Department of Agriculture (USDA). Knowing your farmer is the best way to know the farming practices that were in play to bring that food to your table.

COOKING TIMES

While we wish we could say that we personally tested every recipe in or on every kind of oven there is, sadly we don't have the means or time to do that. Most of our recipe development and testing was done on a gas stove (with burners that ranged from about 2 inches to 5 inches in diameter) and in an electric oven. We can tell you that it takes our oven exactly 11 minutes and 49 seconds to preheat to 350°F. Our recipes do not factor in preheating of the oven time. In pressure cooking, if we've used our Instant Pot to sauté something first, then heat the contents to pressure, it takes about 5 minutes to reach high pressure. Going from cold to high pressure can take anywhere from 5 to 15 minutes (it depends on how much food is in the pressure cooker and whether it is already hot—the food or the pressure cooker).

SEASONINGS

Some people like really salty things. Others are under doctor's orders to lower their salt consumption. We probably tend to go lighter on the salt than some, but heavier than others would want. Generally speaking, it's pretty challenging to remove salt from an already cooked meal. Always err on the side of less salt and season to your particular tastes at the table.

WASHING

Always wash all fruits and vegetables. Even if something says "prewashed," you may wish to wash it again just to be certain it is as clean as possible.

A few notes on washing:

- **Mushrooms:** Because they are super absorbent, we prefer to wipe them clean with a wet cloth or paper towel rather than immerse them in water.

- **Leafy green vegetables:** A salad spinner is the easiest way to clean and dry them.

- **Leeks:** Leeks are grown in sandy soil and tend to hold a lot of dirt. To get them clean, cut off the root end and the dark green tops and compost those or save for your next batch of stock. You can then either halve the stalks lengthwise and swish around in a bowl of water so the dirt falls to the bottom; or you can halve lengthwise then crosswise as you would use for your recipe, and then rinse in cold water, drain, and use.

- **Fish, meat, and poultry:** Lots of recipes and even some famous chefs call for rinsing your fish, meat, or poultry before cooking. However, most food safety experts—including the USDA—advise against this practice due to the potential risk of spreading harmful bacteria. We're going to side with the food safety experts here and suggest that you not rinse first. (One less thing to have to do!). We do suggest patting dry any protein— especially if you're going for a crispy skin on some poultry or fish or you want a nice browned exterior on some steak.

MEASUREMENTS

If we say to chop something into ¼-inch pieces and you chop it into ½-inch pieces, chances are that everything is going to be just fine. Some people get really spun up about exact measurements—and don't get us wrong, if you're doing some bread baking or mastering a soufflé or trying to get a 4.0 in culinary school, these things can be vital. However, you can tweak about 99 percent of the things in our recipes a bit to your liking.

When measuring dry goods, such as flours (coconut, almond), the scoop and scrape method is preferred and what we use—dip your measuring cup or spoon into what you are measuring, and level the top with a flat edge to be even with the top of the cup or spoon. For liquids, use a glass measuring cup, and fill to the appropriate line.

SERVING SIZES

What exactly is a serving? Is it 4 ounces of protein? Is it ½ cup or 1 cup or 2 cups of spinach? Is a serving for Charles (who is six foot three) supposed to be the same amount as for Scott, our three-year-old? Chances are likely not. Not to mention the fact that if someone was intermittent fasting or hitting the gym pretty hard they might be needing a lot more food at that meal than someone else. To provide some guidelines, we generally figure that for meals that include protein, one serving is 4 to 6 ounces per person. Very often we'll say a range of how many people a recipe might serve or what volume of something a recipe yields. If 4 ounces of chicken is an appetizer-size portion for you, then take that into consideration when looking at a recipe's yield. It's not an exact science, so use your own common sense.

SUBSTITUTIONS

We could write an entire book on substitutions. (Thankfully there are other, way smarter people who have already done that. Check out David Joachim's *The Food Substitutions Bible* if you like to geek out on that kind of stuff.) Here's the thing: The recipes in this book would get really confusing if we wrote "or, or, or, or" for all the things you could substitute (though we do like to suggest some variations to help you in the creativity department). Generally speaking, most of our recipes lend themselves exceptionally well to your own interpretation, and we hope you will tweak things and try out what you prefer. Don't like bell peppers in a recipe? Try something of comparable cooking time that suits your fancy. Prefer rib eye over T-bone steak? No problem. Don't have coconut flour for the Morning Glory Muffins Revisited (page 233)? STOP. Baking is almost universally the one exception to the "substitute as you see fit" rule. Things like almond, coconut, and tapioca flour all have different properties and different characteristics, and making willy-nilly substitutions could be disastrous. Now, if you would rather use yellow squash over zucchini in those same muffins, that would not be a problem. But when it comes to the science of baking, one must either know what one is doing or be prepared for an outcome that might not be as intended.

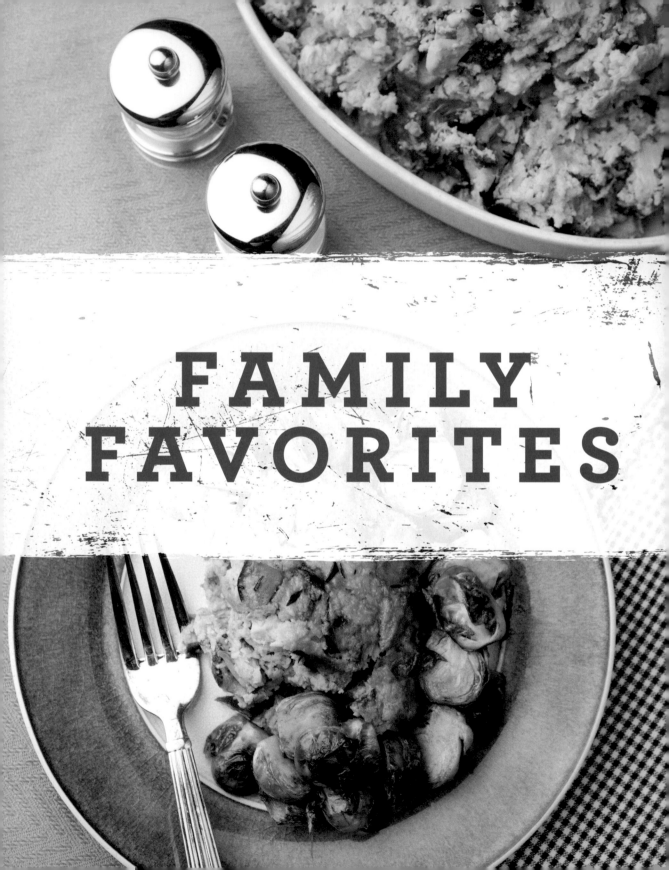

FAMILY FAVORITES

These are the recipes that our family never seems to grow tired of, and they make frequent appearances on our dinner table.

Basic Roast Chicken 26

Spicy Sausage Gumbo 28

Basic Poached Chicken 31

BBQ Meatloaf Roll 32

Celery Root and Cauliflower Soup 35

Green Enchiladas 36

Shrimp and Grits II 38

All-American Burgers 41

Chicken Mushroom Rice Casserole 42

Roasted Pork Tenderloin with Apples and Fennel 45

Chicken Nuggets Redux 47

Beef Filet with Yuca Hash Browns 51

Meat Mixes 52

    Meat Mix #1: Italian 52

    Meat Mix #2: Asian 54

    Meat Mix #3: Southwestern 55

    Meat Mix #4: Veggie 56

Wonton-ish Soup 58

Ginger-Garlic Chicken with Cilantro Sauce 60

Kung Pao Chicken 62

Pork Chops with Butternut Squash Noodles and Guajillo Sauce 65

Homemade Chorizo Patties 68

Basic Roast Chicken

Whole roast chicken screams comfort food to us. There is something about coming home to the smell of a chicken in the oven—it's almost Thanksgiving-like but without all the effort of the huge Thanksgiving meal. A whole roast chicken is great for many reasons—not just because it's delicious. For starters, it makes use of the whole chicken—and since most of your local farmers aren't selling you boneless, skinless chicken breasts, this is a great way to use all the parts. Second, the carcass can—and should!—be used to make chicken stock (see the recipe on page 209). The secret best part of this recipe? The roasted radishes. You'll find yourself wishing you had roasted more!

SERVES 4 TO 6 / PREP TIME: 10 MINUTES / TOTAL TIME: 1 HOUR 10 MINUTES

1 onion, cut into wedges

4 to 5 whole carrots, peeled (greens removed if they came with them)

½ pound asparagus, tough ends removed

1 cup radishes, halved lengthwise

2 to 3 cloves garlic, minced

2 tablespoons extra-virgin olive oil

1 4-to-5-pound whole chicken

1 tablespoon salt

1 teaspoon black pepper

1. Preheat the oven to 450°F.

2. Place the vegetables and garlic on a large rimmed baking sheet or in a large roasting pan and toss with 1 tablespoon of the olive oil. Leave a few onion pieces in the center, and push all the remaining vegetables to the perimeter of the pan.

3. Use paper towels to pat the chicken dry. Place the chicken breast side up in the center of the pan. Tuck the wing tips under the chicken and tie the legs together (optional but helps with even cooking). Drizzle with the remaining 1 tablespoon olive oil.

4. Season the chicken and vegetables with the salt and pepper.

5. Place the pan in the oven and reduce the temperature to 400°F. Bake until an instant-read thermometer inserted in the thickest part of the thigh (being careful not to hit the bone) registers 165°F, about 1 hour.

6. Remove from the oven and allow to rest for 10 minutes before carving and serving.

✳ VARIATIONS: *There are so many ways you can switch up the seasonings and/or the vegetables for this dish. Try rubbing some garlic-rosemary paste all over and under the chicken skin, and select potatoes as your vegetable. Or sprinkle 1 tablespoon paprika (sweet or smoked) over the chicken and roast with sweet potatoes and parsnips. Or season the chicken simply with salt and pepper, roast with your favorite vegetables, and drizzle with just a tiny bit of truffle oil after it's done cooking. That might be our favorite way!*

Spicy Sausage Gumbo

Ask any person of Cajun or Creole heritage how they define gumbo, and you're likely to get a whole host of responses, coupled with some great family stories. This recipe, loosely based on our family's gumbo, creates a thick and robust stew. (Oh, and before we ruffle too many Cajuns' feathers: Charles's mom hails from Alabama, where it's quite common to add tomatoes to gumbo. Some folks swear this is sacrilege. If you prefer to omit the tomatoes, go ahead and do so.) While many iterations of gumbo involve shellfish (and in our family we have a hard time saying no to gumbo that includes freshly cleaned and picked Mobile Bay crabs), we wanted to come up with something for those times when you don't have the extra hours to pick crab.

SERVES 6 TO 8 / PREP TIME: 5 MINUTES / TOTAL TIME: 30 MINUTES

2 pounds bulk pork sausage

2 tablespoons coconut oil

1 medium sweet onion, diced

3 cloves garlic, minced

2 teaspoons Cajun Spice Mix (page 225), or use store-bought

¼ cup coconut flour

3 cups diced, canned tomatoes

4 cups chicken stock, store-bought or homemade (page 209)

3 cups chopped okra

2 cups riced cauliflower (see "How to Make Cauliflower Rice," page 30)

1 bunch green onions, sliced

1. In a large Dutch oven, cook the sausage over medium-high heat. Use a wooden spoon to break up the sausage into small bits as it cooks. Transfer to a large bowl when cooked through, about 5 minutes.

2. Return the Dutch oven to the heat and add the coconut oil. Add the onion and cook for a few minutes, until translucent. Add the garlic and Cajun seasoning, stirring frequently for about a minute.

3. Add the coconut flour and stir to coat all the onions. As the mixture begins to brown, add the tomatoes and cook for another 2 minutes. Pour in the chicken stock along with the okra and cauliflower. Cover and bring to a quick boil.

4. Once boiling, return the sausage to the pan, reduce the heat to a simmer, cover, and cook for 10 minutes. Serve with a healthy garnish of green onion.

VARIATIONS: *There are quite a few common substitutions you can use for this recipe. Any type of bulk sausage (chorizo, country, Italian) can be used and we encourage you to play around with what tastes best to you. We love using seafood stock for this recipe and occasionally swap the cauliflower with shredded cabbage.*

HOW TO MAKE CAULIFLOWER RICE

Cauliflower "rice" is one of our favorite Paleo substitutions and for good reason—cauliflower packs a much bigger nutritional punch than regular rice—and it's so much quicker to cook! It's so popular that stores like Trader Joe's are now selling packaged frozen cauliflower rice. While already riced cauliflower is convenient and makes less of a mess in the kitchen, making your own is easy and much more gentle on the budget. Bonus: You can freeze your own too.

TO MAKE THE RICE: Remove and discard the green leaves and the core from a head of cauliflower. Chop the florets into small pieces. Working in a few batches, add some of the florets to a food processor and pulse until you have a rice-like consistency. Alternately, you can also use the shredding blade on the processor to create the rice. If you don't have a food processor, a box grater is a good substitute, though you'll probably have a lot of cauliflower bits all over the kitchen to clean up when you're done.

Although fresh cauliflower rice freezes well, we do not recommend making rice out of store-bought, frozen cauliflower as the texture is not quite right.

TO FREEZE: Place the raw cauliflower rice in a resealable freezer bag or two. Remove as much of the air as possible, seal, and freeze. You can also spread the riced cauliflower onto a parchment-lined baking sheet and freeze that way so it doesn't clump as much, and then place it in a resealable freezer bag.

To serve, we will oftentimes use raw cauliflower rice in place of regular rice, but we know some people prefer a cooked cauliflower rice. You can either steam the rice in the microwave or sauté it with a tablespoon or two of coconut oil (or other fat), along with a few tablespoons of chicken stock.

Basic Poached Chicken

Long-touted as the health spa–preferred method of cooking chicken, poaching is a nonfat way of cooking protein that is quick, easy, and *almost* foolproof as it relates to not overcooking, though it is possible to overcook, which is why we strongly recommend an instant-read meat thermometer to help prevent dry, tough poultry. Then again, we strongly recommend an instant-read thermometer for almost any method of cooking meat. Your poaching liquid can be flavor-enhanced by any aromatics of your choosing (see the ingredient list for some ideas). Poaching gently infuses the chicken with the flavors of the poaching liquid, so think about how you'll be using the chicken to determine what aromatics might be best.

YIELD VARIES / PREP TIME: 5 MINUTES / TOTAL TIME: 30 MINUTES

2 pounds or more bone-in or boneless chicken breasts or thighs

Chicken stock, store-bought or homemade (page 209), or water (enough to cover the chicken)

2 teaspoons kosher salt

Any aromatics of your choosing (fresh herbs, onions, garlic cloves, peppercorns, etc.)

1. In a large Dutch oven or deep skillet with a lid, arrange the chicken skin side up and add enough stock to cover the chicken by at least 1 inch. Add the salt and aromatics.

2. Bring the stock to a low boil over medium-high heat. Reduce the heat to a simmer, and cook the chicken for about 10 minutes.

3. Remove from the heat, cover, and allow to sit until an instant-read thermometer registers 165°F, 15 to 20 minutes (see Note).

4. Shred, store, or eat the chicken. The poaching liquid can be saved, strained, reduced, and used as a stock.

NOTE: *Some people swear that you should let the chicken cool in the poaching liquid. This is not advisable from a food safety perspective as harmful bacteria can start to grow. The USDA recommends minimizing the amount of time food spends in "the danger zone" (between 40° and 140°F), noting that food that spends more than 2 hours in that zone should be discarded.*

BBQ Meatloaf Roll

This recipe is great to prep ahead of time and store in the refrigerator, so all you need to do is pop it in the oven for supper when you're ready to eat. Serve over mashed cauliflower, potatoes, or yuca.

SERVES 6 TO 8 / PREP TIME: 15 MINUTES / TOTAL TIME: 1 HOUR

1 pound ground beef

1 pound bulk pork sausage

1 medium egg

1 tablespoon garlic powder

1 teaspoon kosher salt

½ teaspoon black pepper

½ teaspoon chipotle powder

3 tablespoons fat (butter, ghee, or coconut oil)

1 medium onion, chopped

1 clove garlic, minced

¼ cup beef stock

3 tablespoons tomato paste

1 tablespoon apple cider vinegar

1 tablespoon yellow mustard

½ teaspoon Tabasco sauce

4 cups tightly packed spinach

1. Preheat the oven to 375°F.
2. In a large bowl, combine the beef, sausage, egg, garlic powder, salt, pepper, and chipotle powder and mix thoroughly.
3. Using your hands or a rolling pin, form a 9 x 13-inch rectangle of meat on parchment paper, making sure the thickness is fairly even, and place in the refrigerator to chill while assembling the other ingredients.
4. In a skillet, heat 2 tablespoons of the fat over medium. Add the onion and garlic and cook for 5 minutes, until the onions soften.
5. Measure out ¼ cup of the sautéed onions and garlic and transfer to a food processor. Add the remaining 1 tablespoon fat to the processor along with the beef stock, tomato paste, vinegar, mustard, and Tabasco and pulse to make a paste.
6. Add the spinach to the skillet with the remaining onions and garlic and cook over medium heat until wilted.
7. Remove the meat roll from the refrigerator and brush some of the paste on top.
8. Spread the sautéed veggies out across two-thirds of the meat. Roll the meat up lengthwise and press the edges/flaps down to enclose all the filling.
9. Transfer the loaf to a 9 x 13-inch baking dish and liberally coat with the remainder of the paste.
10. Bake until an instant-read thermometer registers 145°F, 30 to 45 minutes.

✱ VARIATIONS: *We've tried this recipe using beef, pork, venison, and lamb. Feel free to play with whatever you have on hand. If you happen to have some of our No-Cook Barbecue Sauce (page 216) lying around, you can shave off a few minutes from this recipe by using it in place of the paste. Try swapping out the spinach for dandelion greens or asparagus.*

Celery Root and Cauliflower Soup

Celery root—also known as celeriac—isn't winning any beauty contests. Never ones to judge a book or a vegetable by its cover, we are big fans of this winter root and seize the opportunity to grab some in those colder months. Celery root tastes like a cross between celery and parsley. Though celery and celery root are from the same botanical family, they are not in fact from the same plant. Here we pair the root with the sweetness from an apple and the almost nutty flavor of cauliflower to create a wintertime soup.

SERVES 6 TO 8 / PREP TIME: 10 MINUTES / TOTAL TIME: 30 MINUTES

2 apples (any variety), peeled and cored

1 tablespoon olive oil or coconut oil

1 sweet onion, chopped

1 teaspoon celery seeds

2 celery roots (about 1 pound each), peeled and cut into ½-inch cubes

½ head cauliflower, coarsely chopped (about 3 cups)

5 cups chicken stock, store-bought or homemade (page 209)

½ cup full-fat coconut milk or heavy cream

Salt and white pepper

1. Chop 1½ of the apples into large chunks. Set aside ½ apple for garnish.

2. In a large Dutch oven or soup pot, heat the oil over medium heat. When shimmering, add the onion and sauté until translucent, 4 to 5 minutes. Sprinkle in the celery seeds and stir.

3. Increase the heat to medium-high, add the celery root, cauliflower, chicken stock, and apple chunks and bring to a boil. Reduce the heat to medium-low, cover, and simmer until the celery root, cauliflower, and apple are softened, 10 to 15 minutes.

4. Remove from the heat and stir in the coconut milk, seasoning to taste with the salt and pepper.

5. Working in batches, puree the soup in a blender (see Note).

6. Ladle the soup into bowls. Slice the remaining ½ apple and use the apple slices to garnish your soup bowls.

NOTE: *You can use an immersion blender for this recipe, but the soup won't be as creamy.*

VARIATIONS: *Some sautéed fennel adds a great anise-like punch, or some white potatoes make this soup even creamier. Topped with cooked chicken or seared scallops, this makes a great one-dish meal.*

Green Enchiladas

For those on a low-carb adventure, finding something easy to use as tortilla wrappers can be challenging. While you can buy some Paleo tortillas in the store these days, we're about upping our veggie content whenever we can. Collard greens—a staple in the South—make a great wrapper for these enchiladas. They're durable, full of vitamins and nutrients, and far less expensive than any store-bought wraps. Try these out next time you have a hankering for enchiladas!

SERVES 3 TO 4 / PREP TIME: 15 MINUTES / TOTAL TIME: 30 MINUTES

2 tablespoons fat (ghee, coconut oil, or lard)

2 poblano peppers, stems removed, seeded and chopped

1 medium onion, minced

3 cloves garlic, minced

1½ teaspoons ground cumin

1 pound boneless, skinless chicken breasts or thighs, cut into small chunks or thin strips (or use 1 pound leftover cooked chicken)

¼ cup chopped fresh cilantro

One 4-ounce can green chiles (optional)

Salt and black pepper

2 cups salsa verde, store-bought or homemade (page 219)

8 to 10 large collard green leaves

1. Preheat the oven to 375°F. Bring a large pot of water to a boil.

2. Heat a large skillet over medium-high heat and add the fat. Once shimmering, add the poblano peppers, onion, and garlic and sauté until the onions are translucent, 3 to 5 minutes.

3. Add the cumin and chicken and stir, sautéing until the chicken is cooked through, about 5 minutes more. Transfer the chicken to a cutting board and coarsely chop.

4. Return the chicken to the pan with the vegetables and stir in the cilantro and green chiles (if using). Season with salt and black pepper to taste. Stir in about ½ cup of the salsa verde.

5. To prepare the collard greens, add them to the boiling water and blanch for 30 to 60 seconds, then drain and rinse under cold water.

6. To assemble the enchiladas, cut the bottom of the collard leaf to make a flat edge and trim the sides as appropriate. Place about ⅓ cup of the chicken mixture on a leaf, toward the bottom. Carefully roll up the leaf from the bottom to cover the mixture, fold in the sides, then continue rolling to create the enchilada. Place in an 8 x 8-inch baking pan. Repeat until all the filling is used.

7. Place the enchiladas in the oven and bake for 10 minutes to heat everything through.

Shrimp and Grits II

Our first shrimp and "grits" (we use that term loosely) recipe is what got the whole notion of writing a cookbook started. While we liked our first attempt, we also like reinventing recipes every now and then. The grits in this recipe have more almond meal and less cauliflower than in our original, and we actually took bacon out of the shrimp recipe. We know, that may detract points with some of you, but we think you'll be happy even without the salty, bacony goodness. The shrimp recipe is thanks in part to chef Chris Hall.

SERVES 6 TO 8 AS A MAIN COURSE / PREP TIME: 15 MINUTES / TOTAL TIME: 30 MINUTES

FOR THE "GRITS"

1 cup chicken stock, store-bought or homemade (page 209)

1 cup almond meal (see Notes)

4 cups riced cauliflower (see "How to Make Cauliflower Rice," page 30)

FOR THE SHRIMP

2 tablespoons oil (olive, coconut, or avocado)

½ medium sweet onion, diced

1 red bell pepper, diced

1 green bell pepper, diced

2 cloves garlic, minced

2 pounds shrimp, peeled and deveined

1 teaspoon hot sauce (optional; we like Frank's)

1 cup heavy cream or coconut milk

Juice of 2 lemons

2 tablespoons Old Bay seasoning (see Notes)

Salt and black pepper

1. To make the grits: In a medium saucepan, combine the stock and 2 cups water. Bring to a boil over high heat.

2. Slowly pour in the almond meal, whisking to keep lumps from forming.

3. Stir in the cauliflower and bring the mixture to a simmer. Simmer, stirring frequently, for about 10 minutes, until the cauliflower is softened and you have a creamy grits-like consistency. Cover and keep warm until ready to serve.

4. To make the shrimp: In a large saucepan, heat the oil over medium-high heat. When the oil is shimmering, add the onion and bell peppers and cook until they begin to soften, 3 to 4 minutes. Add the garlic and cook for 1 minute. Add the shrimp and sauté until they just begin to turn pink.

5. Deglaze the pan with the hot sauce (if using) and heavy cream. Add the lemon juice and Old Bay, and season with salt and black pepper to taste. Serve over the "grits."

NOTES: *Almond meal is typically coarser than almond flour and usually involves the skins of the almonds. In this recipe you want the almond meal to be coarse, so using finely ground almond flour would not achieve the same result. Should you need to be nut-free, you can omit the almond meal and just use all cauliflower with a 1:1 ratio.*

Old Bay seasoning is a staple in many kitchens across the country, especially those in the Mid-Atlantic area. The exact Old Bay recipe is evidently top secret, and while making a suitable substitute is possible, it would require about 18 or so herbs and spices (according to McCormick, the manufacturer of Old Bay). Instead, if you don't have Old Bay, use 1 tablespoon celery salt, and pinches of black pepper, paprika, and mustard powder.

All-American Burgers

Burgers are on our menu almost weekly. They reheat wonderfully and are a great, portable source of protein. While bacon as a fixing is delicious, we love incorporating it right into the burger. Pine Street Market in Atlanta makes our favorite bacon, and we love their "bacon burger" mix—bacon, ground with a meat grinder, combined with ground pork. While burgers made just with bacon burger are possible and quite indulgent, we like to combine a pound of bacon burger with a pound of ground beef. Because this recipe uses bacon and ground pork, you'll want to cook the burgers more toward the well done side to be safe. Serve in lettuce wraps or on tomato slices with any other toppings you would like.

MAKES 6 TO 8 BURGERS / PREP TIME: 10 MINUTES / TOTAL TIME: 25 MINUTES

1 pound ground beef

½ pound ground bacon (see Notes)

½ pound ground pork (see Notes)

½ cup minced sweet onion

½ cup finely chopped portobello mushrooms

1 tablespoon garlic powder

2 teaspoons ancho chile powder

Sea salt

1. Preheat the grill to 400°F.
2. In a large bowl, combine all the ingredients (except the salt) and mix thoroughly.
3. Form the meat into 6 to 8 patties and sprinkle each side with salt.
4. Grill the burgers over direct heat for 3 to 4 minutes per side. Give the burgers an additional 2 to 3 minutes of indirect heat to cook through. Be sure to allow them a few minutes to rest once you've pulled them off the grill.

NOTES: *Alternatively, you could substitute the ground bacon and ground pork for 1 pound of any ground sausage. Burgers are a great place to hide some liver for the kids . . . or for us! Take a few ounces of raw liver and chop it up as finely as possible. Mix into the meat and you won't even know it's there!*

Chicken Mushroom Rice Casserole

Charles's sister made a variation of this dish as a Thanksgiving side and it was the hit of the meal. We think that cheese adds a special something, so if you tolerate dairy, we highly recommend adding some—though even without it, this still ranks as one of our favorites. Adding chicken makes this a great one-dish meal that is the perfect comfort food and a wonderful casserole to have stashed in the freezer. This one takes its inspiration from a dish in Heidi Swanson's cookbook *Super Natural Every Day*.

SERVES 4 TO 6 / PREP TIME: 10 MINUTES / TOTAL TIME: 1 HOUR

2 tablespoons butter (or coconut or olive oil), plus more for greasing

1 medium onion, chopped

½ pound assorted mushrooms (we like a mix of shiitakes, baby bellas, and button mushrooms), cleaned and chopped

3 cloves garlic, minced

1 teaspoon fresh tarragon

1 teaspoon fresh thyme

1 teaspoon salt

½ teaspoon black pepper

½ head cauliflower, riced (about 4 cups; see "How to Make Cauliflower Rice," page 30)

3 large eggs

1 cup heavy cream or full-fat coconut milk

2 cups cooked chicken, shredded or chopped into bite-size chunks

½ cup shredded Gruyére cheese (optional)

1. Preheat the oven to 350°F. Grease a 9 x 13-inch baking dish (or another shape of similar capacity).

2. Heat a large skillet over medium heat and add the butter. When the butter has melted (being careful not to burn), add the onion and mushrooms and sauté until the onions are translucent and the mushrooms have softened, 5 to 7 minutes.

3. Stir in the garlic, tarragon, thyme, salt, pepper, and cauliflower and sauté for a minute more.

4. Meanwhile, in a small bowl, whisk together the eggs and cream.

5. Transfer the mushroom-cauliflower mixture to a large bowl and stir in the egg-cream mixture. Fold in the chicken and stir to combine well.

6. Scrape the mixture into the prepared baking dish and cover with foil (see Note).

7. Bake for 30 minutes, then remove the foil. Top with the cheese (if using) and bake, uncovered, until slightly browned and the casserole is set, 20 minutes longer.

VARIATIONS: *For some extra greens, add in 1 cup chopped frozen spinach. If you are a mustard fan, mix in 2 tablespoons Dijon or spicy brown mustard. If you need a vegetarian dish, omit the chicken. There are so many other ways in which you can vary this recipe—give your own version a shot.*

Roast Pork Tenderloin with Apples and Fennel

Pork tenderloin is a favorite among those who want quick and easy dinnertime solutions. It's lean and tender and can be easily sliced into medallions for a short cooking time to help make dinner come together super fast. Here we take the tenderloin, give it a quick exterior sear, and then roast it along with some complementary vegetables and fruits. Easy enough for a weeknight, tasty enough for company!

SERVES 6 TO 8 / PREP TIME: 10 MINUTES / TOTAL TIME: 30 MINUTES, PLUS RESTING TIME

1 large fennel bulb, sliced (1½ to 2 cups)

3 Granny Smith or other tart apples, cored and sliced

1 onion, sliced

3 tablespoons olive oil, avocado oil, or other fat

1 tablespoon fresh rosemary, minced

2 sprigs fresh thyme leaves, chopped

2 cloves garlic, minced

1 teaspoon salt

½ teaspoon black pepper

2 pounds pork tenderloin, trimmed of silver skin (two 1-pound tenderloins; see Note)

1. Preheat the oven to 450°F.

2. On a large rimmed baking sheet, toss the fennel, apples, and onion with 2 tablespoons of the oil. Place in the oven for 10 minutes.

3. While the vegetables roast, in a small bowl, combine the rosemary, thyme, garlic, salt, and pepper. Coat the pork with the seasoning mix.

4. Heat a large skillet over medium-high heat. Add the remaining 1 tablespoon oil and when shimmering, add the pork. Sear until slightly browned on one side, 3 to 4 minutes. Flip and repeat on the other side.

5. Remove the pan of vegetables from the oven and clear space in the middle for the pork tenderloins. Return to the oven and continue roasting until an instant-read thermometer inserted in the pork registers 145°F, about 10 minutes longer.

NOTE: *Make sure you get pork tenderloin, not pork loin! Pork loin is much thicker, and typically needs a low, slow cooking method to get the meat tender.*

Chicken Nuggets Redux

Lots of folks on the Internet have some great knock-off chicken nuggets recipes (that taste mighty similar to a certain fast-food item from an establishment known for its advertising campaigns filled with cow antics) that we've enjoyed trying out and tinkering with. Not too long ago, we realized that we had some chicken brining in pickle juice for this recipe, but we had failed to pick up eggs at our farmers' market. We looked in the fridge and saw that we had some of our homemade mayo (page 211) and since mayo is mostly eggs anyway, we decided to give that a shot for the "batter" to help the coating adhere. We swear the mayo coating helped these retain their moisture and were even more delicious. If you don't have mayo on hand, just use two lightly beaten eggs in step 2. We like to use a large, deep Dutch oven to cook this recipe. For starters, it helps minimize the oil splatter on the stove, and using cast iron helps make the heat distribution a bit more even. Serve the nuggets with our honey mustard (page 212) and/or No-Cook Barbecue Sauce (page 216).

SERVES 6 TO 8 (OR ONE HUNGRY TODDLER) / PREP TIME: 10 MINUTES, PLUS MARINATING TIME / TOTAL TIME: 30 MINUTES

2 pounds boneless, skinless chicken breasts or thighs, cut into bite-size nuggets of even size

⅓ cup dill pickle juice (we like Bubbies brand)

½ cup mayonnaise, store-bought (Paleo-friendly is ideal) or homemade (page 211)

½ cup coconut oil, divided

½ cup almond flour (see Note)

½ cup arrowroot starch/flour or tapioca flour

1 teaspoon sweet paprika

1 teaspoon garlic powder

½ teaspoon onion powder

¾ teaspoon salt

¼ teaspoon black pepper

1. At least 15 minutes before cooking, but as long as a day ahead, place the chicken pieces and pickle juice in a large resealable plastic bag, and mix to ensure even distribution of the pickle juice. Refrigerate until ready to proceed to step 2.

2. When ready to cook the nuggets, drain the chicken pieces in a colander. Return the chicken to the bag and add the mayonnaise, massaging the bag to evenly coat the pieces with the mayo.

3. Heat a large Dutch oven over medium-high heat. Add ¼ cup of the oil and heat until shimmering.

(recipe continues)

(continued from previous page)

4. While the oil is heating, in a large bowl, combine the almond flour, arrowroot starch/
flour, paprika, garlic powder, onion powder, salt, and pepper. Add the chicken pieces to the
mixture and coat well.

5. When the oil reaches temperature, add several pieces of the chicken (being sure not to
crowd the pan). After cooking about 3 minutes on the first side to a golden brown color,
use tongs to flip to the other side and continue until cooked through, 3 to 4 minutes longer.

6. Transfer to a plate lined with paper towels. Continue cooking the chicken in batches,
adding the additional ¼ cup oil if needed (though you'll need to let it come to temperature).

NOTE: *If you're nut-free, replace the almond flour with an equal amount of arrowroot starch/flour or tapioca flour.*

HONEY MUSTARD SAUCE (PAGE 212)

Beef Filet with Yuca Hash Browns

This is our version of "steak and potatoes." We love to incorporate yuca root here and there as it's a great source of starchier carbohydrates. You'll be amazed at how this fibrous and incredibly tough root turns into a soft and buttery addition to any recipe.

SERVES 3 TO 4 / PREP TIME: 25 MINUTES / TOTAL TIME: 45 TO 50 MINUTES

1 medium yuca root, peeled, tough center removed, and cut into ½-inch cubes (see Notes)

1 pound beef filet, cut into 4 steaks (see Notes)

½ teaspoon kosher salt

¼ teaspoon black pepper

1 tablespoon bacon fat or oil

2 tablespoons butter

1 teaspoon fresh thyme

1 teaspoon fresh rosemary, minced

1. Bring a pot of water to a boil. Add the yuca and cook until fork-tender, 15 to 20 minutes. Drain and allow to cool.

2. While the yuca is cooking, dry the filets and sprinkle with the salt and pepper.

3. In a large cast-iron skillet, heat the bacon fat until it is just about to smoke, then add the filets. Cook for 1 to 2 minutes on each side and remove to a cutting board to rest.

4. While the meat is resting, heat the skillet over medium-high heat, then add in the butter and yuca. Cook for about 7 minutes, stirring at least once, to brown the yuca. When the yuca is done, sprinkle with the thyme and rosemary.

5. Serve each filet with a helping of yuca hash browns.

NOTES: *We like to keep some preboiled yuca on hand in our refrigerator or freezer, which makes recipes like this much faster. If you are going to boil the root yourself, be sure to remove the tough middle part, known as the spindle. Some stores stock frozen, already peeled yuca, which makes life a little easier.*

Beef or venison is best with this household favorite.

Meat Mixes

Meat mixes are so versatile and make for a great something to have on hand in the freezer. Once you've mastered the meat mixes of your choosing, you'll have something that can be served on its own as meatballs, formed into meatloaves, even transformed into burgers. Make up your own meat mixes and see what you come up with!

Meat Mix #1: Italian

Chef Chris Hall is many things to our family—"Uncle Chris" to the kids, dear friend to both of us—not to mention one heck of a chef and businessman, with one of the biggest, most generous hearts. A few years back, I strong-armed Chris into coming along with me to Camp Sunshine (the pediatric oncology camp in Georgia) to teach a cooking class to the teenagers. This recipe is based on his grandma's Italian-style meatballs he taught the kids—proving to anyone and everyone that you don't need his restaurant's $2 million kitchen to make really amazing-tasting food. It's all about the skilled hands of the chef. We always make at least two pounds of this mixture as it goes fast in our house! **—JULIE**

MAKES ABOUT 50 (1-OUNCE) MEATBALLS / PREP TIME: 15 MINUTES / TOTAL TIME: 35 MINUTES

2 pounds ground beef

½ pound bacon, finely chopped

1 onion, minced

¼ cup chopped Italian (flat-leaf) parsley

1 tablespoon minced garlic

1 tablespoon dried oregano

½ teaspoon fennel seeds

½ teaspoon crushed red pepper

3 large eggs

1 teaspoon salt

1 teaspoon black pepper

1. In a large bowl, mix together all the ingredients (we prefer to use our hands). Follow the cooking instructions on page 57 for your desired preparation.

2. Serve with 5- Ingredient Tomato Sauce (page 214) or tomato sauce of your choosing and over zucchini noodles, if you prefer.

Meat Mix #2: Asian

It's been a long time since I've had Asian dumplings of the dim sum kind. Mostly because last time I had them I felt so terrible after. That said, I have fantastic memories of some dim sum outings while living in Los Angeles, and some melt-in-your-mouth shumai. This meat mix is great on its own as meatballs, and also makes for a wonderful filling for zucchini, or yellow or even some winter squash (like acorn or delicata); basically this is great in any other vegetable you wish to stuff. Serve the meatballs with Asian Dipping Sauce (below) or use as the dumplings for our Wonton-ish Soup (page 58).   —JULIE

MAKES 24 (1-INCH) MEATBALLS / PREP TIME: 10 MINUTES / TOTAL TIME: 30 TO 40 MINUTES

1 pound ground pork

2 ounces fresh shiitake mushrooms, stems discarded, caps finely chopped (about ½ cup)

1-inch piece fresh ginger, peeled and finely grated or minced

2 garlic cloves, minced

3 green onions, finely chopped

1 tablespoon coconut aminos (or gluten-free soy sauce if you tolerate soy)

2 teaspoons fish sauce (omit if using gluten-free soy sauce)

1½ teaspoons sesame oil

1 teaspoon unseasoned rice vinegar

½ teaspoon salt

¼ teaspoon baking soda

In a large bowl, mix together all the ingredients (we prefer to use our hands). Follow the cooking instructions for your desired preparation on page 57.

Asian Dipping Sauce

Serve with Asian meatballs.

MAKES ABOUT ½ CUP SAUCE

¼ cup unseasoned rice vinegar

2 tablespoons coconut aminos

1 teaspoon fish sauce

½ teaspoon sesame oil

1 teaspoon minced fresh ginger

1 teaspoon sambal oelek, Sriracha, or other hot sauce (optional)

In a bowl, combine all the ingredients well.

Meat Mix #3: Southwestern

We are big fans of Southwestern flavors. Basically anything that offers some bit of a kick (poblanos, chipotles, etc.) mixed in with some protein makes our mouths happy.

MAKES 24 (1-INCH) MEATBALLS / PREP TIME: 10 MINUTES / TOTAL TIME: 30 MINUTES

1 pound ground beef (or ½ pound each of beef and venison)

2 tablespoons finely chopped poblano pepper

2 tablespoons finely chopped onion

1 large clove garlic, minced

1 chipotle pepper in adobo sauce, minced, plus 1 teaspoon adobo sauce

1 tablespoon coarsely chopped fresh cilantro

1 large egg

2 teaspoons ground cumin

½ teaspoon salt

In a large bowl, mix together all the ingredients (we prefer to use our hands). Follow the cooking instructions on page 57 for your desired preparation.

VARIATION: *Meatballs—especially ones as flavorful as these Southwestern ones—are a great opportunity to try to hide some liver. Just add in a few tablespoons of raw, finely chopped liver and know you're getting some great nutrients!*

NOTE: *If you don't have or cannot find chipotles in adobo sauce or you don't have some homemade chipotle sauce, use 1 tablespoon tomato paste as a substitute.*

Meat Mix #4: Veggie

This mix is a wonderful way to sneak more vegetables into your family's diet. Feel free to double this recipe (see Note).

MAKES 24 (1-INCH) MEATBALLS / PREP TIME: 10 MINUTES / TOTAL TIME: 30 TO 40 MINUTES

1 pound ground beef (or ½ pound each of beef and venison)

¼ cup shredded carrots

1 tablespoon finely chopped onion

1 tablespoon finely chopped green bell pepper

1 tablespoon finely chopped mushroom

1 tablespoon finely chopped parsnip

1 large clove garlic, finely chopped

1 teaspoon salt (see Note)

½ teaspoon black pepper

½ teaspoon garlic powder

¼ teaspoon paprika

¼ teaspoon chipotle powder

¼ teaspoon cayenne pepper

¼ teaspoon dry thyme

In a large bowl, mix together all the ingredients (we prefer to use our hands). Follow the cooking instructions for your desired preparation on page 57.

NOTE: *Keep a jar of Penzeys Northwoods Fire in your pantry. You may substitute 1 tablespoon for the last seven ingredients in this recipe to save a few minutes of measuring.*

For meatballs:

1. Preheat the oven to 375°F.
2. Form the meat mix into 1-ounce meatballs (about the size of a Ping-Pong ball) and place them on a rimmed baking sheet lined with parchment paper. Bake until cooked through, about 20 minutes.

For mini meatloaves:

1. Preheat the oven to 375°F.
2. Form the meat mix into equally sized loves. (Divide 1 pound meat into 3 or 4 rectangler loaves, or form 2 pounds meat into 6 to 8 loaves.) Place them on a rimmed baking sheet lined with parchment paper.
3. Bake for 20 to 30 minutes or until the internal temperature is 160°F.
4. Allow to rest for 10 minutes before serving.

NOTE: *You can also make these into meatloaf "muffins." Simply grease the wells of a muffin pan with the fat of your choosing, mound the meat mix into the wells (remembering that the meat will shrink some during cooking), and follow the baking instructions for the mini meatloaves.*

For stuffed zucchini appetizer:

1. Preheat the oven to 350°F. Line a rimmed baking sheet with parchment paper.
2. Cut 2 large zucchini (about 1½ to 2 inches in diameter) crosswise into 1-inch pieces.
3. Using a melon baller, scoop out the middle of the zucchini flesh, being careful not to break all the way through the bottom. Fill the well in the middle of the zucchini with a ball of the meat mix. Remember that the meat will shrink during cooking and give off a good amount of liquid.
4. Arrange on the baking sheet and bake until the meat is cooked through, 15 to 20 minutes.

Wonton-ish Soup

If I had to choose one soup that most reminded me of my childhood it would be wonton soup. Yep, even above those Lipton chicken rice noodle soups, even above Top Ramen (though Top Ramen gets prime billing for my college years). Maybe it had to do with the fact that when my mom would get Chinese takeout for us my sister and I would practically dive headfirst into the hot container of soup. It's surprisingly simple as we prepare it here, and I don't think you'll miss the wonton wrappers.   —JULIE

SERVES 4 TO 6 AS MAIN COURSE / PREP TIME: 10 MINUTES / TOTAL TIME: 25 MINUTES

2 quarts chicken stock, store-bought or homemade (page 209)

1 teaspoon coconut aminos

1 teaspoon fish sauce

1 teaspoon sesame oil

2-inch piece fresh ginger, coarsely chopped

2 cloves garlic, smashed

4 green onions, white and green parts cut into 2-inch pieces, plus more for serving

2 tablespoons coconut oil or avocado oil

Asian meatballs (page 54)

1. In a large pot, combine the chicken stock, aminos, fish sauce, sesame oil, ginger, garlic, and green onions and bring to a simmer. Cook for 15 minutes to let the broth infuse with flavor. Using a slotted spoon, fish out the ginger, garlic, and green onions.

2. Meanwhile, form the meat mix into meatballs the size of Ping-Pong balls. Heat a large skillet over medium-high heat and add the oil. When hot, add the meatballs and sauté until cooked through, 3 to 4 minutes per side. (Alternatively, you can bake them in the oven at 375°F for about 15 minutes.)

3. Evenly divide the meatballs among the soup bowls, and ladle broth over each. Top with fresh green onions to serve.

VARIATION: *Want to get in more veggies? Bok choy is very often seen in wonton soup. Add 2 cups roughly chopped bok choy and add it to the pot in step 1 after straining out the ginger, garlic, and green onions, then cook until tender.*

Ginger-Garlic Chicken with Cilantro Sauce

I believe this recipe originally came from *Gourmet* magazine, and my then roommate would serve this dish over cold (cooked) udon or soba noodles. In this version we serve it over your choice of Paleo-friendly noodles, though if you aren't Paleo, you can easily use any noodles of your choosing.

—JULIE

SERVES 6 TO 8 / PREP TIME: 10 MINUTES / TOTAL TIME: 25 MINUTES, PLUS 1 HOUR MARINATING TIME

FOR THE MARINADE

4 cloves garlic, peeled

1 tablespoon coarsely chopped fresh ginger

2 tablespoons unseasoned rice vinegar

2 pounds boneless, skinless chicken breasts or thighs

FOR THE SAUCE

1 cup chicken stock, store-bought or homemade (page 209)

1 cup sprigs fresh cilantro (stems and leaves)

½ cup Italian (flat-leaf) parsley, stems removed

1 tablespoon coconut oil or olive oil

¼ cup unseasoned rice vinegar

Salt and black pepper

FOR SERVING

4 zucchini, julienned or spiralized, or 2 packages of shirataki (Japanese yam) noodles, rinsed (page 67)

4 green onions, thinly sliced

1. To make the marinade: In a small food processor or blender, combine the garlic, ginger, and vinegar and blend. Transfer to a bowl or plastic bag with the chicken. Allow to marinate for up to 1 hour.

2. To make the sauce: In a small saucepan, combine the stock, cilantro, parsley, and oil and bring to a simmer. Simmer for about 1 minute, then remove from the heat. Puree in a blender or food processor. Stir in the rice vinegar and season with salt and pepper to taste.

3. Preheat a grill to high. Grill the chicken over direct heat for about 4 minutes on the first side. Flip only when the chicken easily releases from the grill, then cook until an instant-read thermometer registers 160°F, about 2 minutes more on the second side. Transfer to a plate (where the carryover cooking will bring the temp up to 165°F).

4. To serve: Slice the chicken and place on top of the noodles. Pour the sauce over all and top with the green onions.

Kung Pao Chicken

When I was growing up, my family was into pretty bland Chinese takeout, mostly because my mom didn't like spicy things. As an adult, I realized that I really like spicy food, and was beyond thrilled with the opportunity to try things that made my mouth sizzle a bit—especially in Asian cuisines. Here's one that adds a nice punch to the palate.

—JULIE

SERVES 3 TO 4 / PREP TIME: 15 MINUTES, PLUS MARINATING TIME / TOTAL TIME: 20 MINUTES

FOR THE CHICKEN

1 teaspoon arrowroot or tapioca flour

½ teaspoon salt

1 tablespoon coconut aminos or gluten-free soy sauce

2 teaspoons dry sherry or Chinese rice wine (optional)

1 pound boneless, skinless chicken breasts or thighs, cut into bite-size pieces

FOR THE SAUCE

1 tablespoon coconut aminos or gluten-free oyster sauce

2 teaspoons Sriracha sauce, chili-garlic sauce, or other hot sauce

2 teaspoons unseasoned rice vinegar

1 teaspoon honey or date paste

1 teaspoon sesame oil

FOR THE STIR-FRY

1 tablespoon avocado oil or coconut oil

6 to 8 (to taste) dried red chiles, seeded and cut in half lengthwise

2 cloves garlic, minced

2 teaspoons minced fresh ginger

2 red or green bell peppers, seeded and cut into bite-size pieces

¼ cup unsalted roasted cashews or macadamia nuts

3 green onions, thinly sliced, plus more for garnish

4 cups cauliflower, riced (see "How to Make Cauliflower Rice," page 30)

1. To marinate the chicken: In a glass container with a lid, combine the arrowroot or tapioca flour, salt, coconut aminos, and sherry (if using). Add the chicken to the mixture and allow to marinate for as little as 10 minutes or as long as overnight (refrigerated).
2. To make the sauce: In a bowl, combine the coconut aminos, Sriracha, vinegar, honey, and sesame oil. This can be made a day ahead and kept covered at room temperature.
3. Drain the chicken from the marinade.
4. To make the stir-fry: Preheat a large wok or skillet over high heat. Add the oil and once shimmering add the chiles and cook for about 20 seconds. Add the chicken and stir-fry until almost cooked through, 2 to 3 minutes.

5. Add the garlic, ginger, and bell peppers, stirring to combine. Cook for about 2 minutes to slightly soften the bell peppers.

6. Pour in the sauce, cashews, and green onions and stir to combine. Cook for about 2 minutes more to heat through.

7. Serve over cauliflower rice or any rice, and garnish with the reserved green onion.

VARIATIONS: *You could most certainly use some chopped-up pork or thinly sliced beef in place of the chicken, or some shrimp would be great as well.*

Pork Chops with Butternut Squash Noodles and Guajillo Sauce

The guajillo sauce can be made ahead of time, as it's a lovely condiment all on its own. The squash noodles go great with any protein of your choosing (though we're big fans of pork chops or chicken cutlets). Don't feel like butternut squash noodles? Give this a shot with sweet potatoes or zucchini or any other vegetable noodles. If you would rather serve the noodles and sauce as a side dish, see the variation that follows.

SERVES 3 TO 4 / PREP TIME: 20 MINUTES / TOTAL TIME: 45 MINUTES

FOR THE GUAJILLO SAUCE

4 dried guajillo chile peppers (see Notes)

1 cup boiling water

1 tablespoon fat (coconut oil, lard, or ghee)

½ onion, coarsely chopped

2 cloves garlic, chopped

2 tablespoons tomato paste

1½ cups full-fat coconut milk or heavy cream

1 to 2 teaspoons adobo sauce from canned chipotles (optional)

½ teaspoon dried oregano

½ teaspoon ground cumin

FOR THE PORK AND NOODLES

1 pound boneless or bone-in pork chops, about 1 inch thick

½ teaspoon chipotle powder

Salt and black pepper

2 tablespoons fat (coconut oil, lard, or ghee)

1 medium butternut squash, peeled and spiralized into noodles

1. Make the sauce: Heat a large skillet over medium heat. Add the guajillos, toasting them until just fragrant but not burned. Remove them from the skillet and tear into small pieces, discarding the stems and seeds. Transfer to a small heatproof bowl and cover with the boiling water. Allow to soak for 15 minutes.

2. Meanwhile, add the fat to the skillet and once hot, add the onion and sauté until just translucent. Add the garlic and cook for 1 minute longer.

3. Stir in the tomato paste, coconut milk, adobo sauce (if using), oregano, and cumin. Add the soaked and drained guajillos, and mix well to combine. Bring just to a boil to allow flavors to infuse into the coconut milk.

4. Pour all the contents of the skillet into a blender and puree until smooth (see Notes). Strain the liquid through a fine-mesh sieve, then return to the stove in the skillet. Simmer for 5 minutes to heat through.

(recipe continues)

(continued from previous page)

5. Make the pork chops and noodles: Preheat the oven to 375°F.

6. Pat the pork chops dry and season with the chipotle powder, and salt and black pepper to taste.

7. Heat a large, ovenproof skillet over medium-high heat. When hot, add the fat. Add the pork chops to the skillet and cook until a nice browned exterior has formed, 3 to 4 minutes per side.

8. Remove the pork chops to a plate. Add the noodles and sauce to the skillet and stir. Place the pork chops on top and place the pan in the oven. Bake until the pork chops are cooked through and the noodles have reached your desired doneness, about 10 minutes.

VARIATION: *If you would prefer this as a meat-free side dish, make the guajillo sauce as directed. Then heat a large skillet over medium heat and add 2 tablespoons of fat. Once hot, add the noodles, stirring to combine well. Sauté until the noodles reach your desired doneness, 5 to 10 minutes (we like them a bit on the still crunchy side). Pour the sauce over the noodles and stir all to combine well.*

NOTES: *Guajillos are pretty mild. If you can't find them, use New Mexico or California chiles.*
Always use caution blending hot ingredients in a blender as the heat can cause the liquid to splatter all over your kitchen. We suggest placing a kitchen towel over the top of the blender and using firm pressure to press down on the lid when you start blending.

HOW TO MAKE VEGETABLE NOODLES

Vegetable noodles as a substitute for pasta are a bit of a staple in Paleo and gluten-free families. Plus, the actual act of "spiralizing" is a great way to get the kids involved. We highly recommend a spiralizer gadget, but there is one to meet everyone's budget and storage space requirements. Check the specific instructions for your spiralizer for setup and use, but general spiralizer instructions follow below. You can spiralize apples, potatoes, squash (summer and some winter), celery root, carrots, parsnips, jicama, beets, daikon, and much more!

1. Place a bowl under the end of the spiralizer to catch the noodles.

2. Cut off the stem-root ends of the vegetable, trimming and/or peeling as needed.

3. Firmly secure the vegetable to the prongs and center hold of the spiralizer, making sure it is centered.

4. Using gentle pressure, turn the crank to create the spiralized noodles.

Homemade Chorizo Patties

Just like the Spanish accent is quite different from the Latin American accent, so is the case with Spanish vs. Mexican chorizo. Though named the same thing, the chorizo you'll find in Spain (typically a hard, cured meat) is not what you'll find in Mexico (a bulk sausage of sorts). This recipe is more of what you'd find in Mexico. Our tip is to always be clear on what kind of chorizo your recipe is calling for as it might make a difference (though both are incredibly tasty in our opinion). We sometimes enjoy breakfast for dinner, so some quick-cooking homemade chorizo along with some eggs makes for a speedy supper the whole family will eat.

SERVES 3 TO 4 / PREP TIME: 5 MINUTES / TOTAL TIME: 20 MINUTES

1 pound ground pork (see Notes)

2 large cloves garlic, minced

2 tablespoons chile powder (New Mexican, ancho, etc.)

1 tablespoon sweet paprika

2 teaspoons dried oregano (preferably Mexican)

1 teaspoon cayenne pepper

1 teaspoon ground cumin

1 teaspoon smoked paprika

½ teaspoon ground allspice

½ teaspoon salt

½ teaspoon black pepper

2 tablespoons apple cider vinegar

In a medium bowl, combine all the ingredients, making sure to incorporate all the spices evenly throughout the meat. We find it easiest to use our hands. For the best flavor, we suggest refrigerating the mixture overnight to allow the flavors to combine. (Or freeze until ready to use.)

To cook chorizo patties:
Form the mixture into evenly sized patties. Heat a large cast-iron or stainless steel skillet over medium heat. When hot, add the patties along with ½ cup water, cover, and cook for about 12 to 15 minutes, turning every few minutes, until cooked through (time will depend on the thickness of your patties).

NOTES: *To cook chorizo in bulk form: Heat a large cast-iron skillet over medium high heat. When hot, add the chorizo, use a wooden spoon to break up the sausage, and cook for 8 to 10 minutes, or until cooked through.*

Make sure your pork is not lean pork. If it is, you'll want to add some fat to it—ideally about 2 tablespoons (at least) of some home-ground pork fat or some finely chopped bacon.

FIX AND FORGET

There's something really awesome about throwing together a bunch of ingredients in a slow cooker or in the oven, stepping away from the kitchen, and hours later having a delicious and ready-to-eat meal. Besides, tougher cuts of meat (which happen to be less expensive, typically) usually warrant low and slow cooking, so this makes the best of all worlds. Oh, and if you forgot to fire up the slow cooker, never fear: the Instant Pot (an electric multipurpose cooker, which can serve as a pressure cooker or slow cooker) is our new favorite kitchen appliance, and it helps us when we want the flavor and texture of something that's been cooked for hours but we have only a fraction of that time.

If you do not own a slow cooker or an Instant Pot, these recipes can also be cooked in the oven in a large Dutch oven or similar ovenproof vessel (with a lid). Generally speaking, to replicate the heat settings on a slow cooker, you'll bake at 200°F for low and 250°F for high; the amount of cooking time will be approximately the same.

Carnitas	73
Chile Colorado	74
Kitchen Sink Stew	76
Pork Mole	78
Pork Tinga	80
Pork Con Thuyen	83
Slow Cooker Short Ribs	85
Chicken Verde	86

Carnitas

We know what you're thinking: This big hunk of meat serves only 8 to 10 people? That seems preposterous! Here's the thing: Pork butt (which is actually from the front quarters of the pig—not the derriere) cooks down by as much as 50 percent. Trust us: If you can get your hands on a bigger piece of meat, do it. You can never go wrong (in our opinion) with too much tender, falling-apart pork. This carnitas recipe is as close as we have gotten to the offering of a certain beloved "fast-casual" Mexican chain restaurant. Serve it over cauliflower rice (page 30), shredded cabbage, lettuce, grilled vegetables, and/or topped with pico de gallo (page 218) and a dollop of guacamole to create your own burrito bowl.

SERVES 8 TO 10 / PREP TIME: 5 MINUTES / TOTAL TIME: 4 TO 8 HOURS IN A SLOW COOKER

5 to 6 pounds pork butt (shoulder), preferably bone-in

1 tablespoon kosher or sea salt

2 teaspoons juniper berries

2 teaspoons garlic powder

2 teaspoons ground cumin

1 teaspoon chipotle powder

1 teaspoon black pepper

4 bay leaves

2 sprigs fresh thyme

1. Pat the pork dry with paper towels.
2. In a spice mill or small food processor, combine the salt, juniper berries, garlic powder, cumin, chipotle powder, and pepper and grind for 30 seconds or so, until you have an even mixture.
3. Coat the entire pork butt with the spice mixture and place it the slow cooker with the thyme and bay leaves placed on top (if your pork has a nice fat cap—and we hope it does!—place it fat cap up; see Note).
4. Cover and cook on high for 4 hours or low for 8 hours, until the meat can be easily pulled apart with a fork.
5. Remove the pork from the slow cooker and shred (or use a knife to chop) and serve.

VARIATIONS: *If you want to crisp up the pork in an authentic carnitas fashion, place it on a rimmed baking sheet lined with foil and cook under a high broiler until crispy.*

Juice from an orange is a great flavor to add to the slow cooker. And while we particularly like the flavor juniper berries bring, if you can't find them, feel free to omit them. The taste won't be quite the same, but it will still be delicious.

NOTE: *Don't have a slow cooker? Bake it in the oven at 225°F for 8 hours in a Dutch oven (which helps retain moisture). You want the internal temperature to reach 195°F. Anything less than that and the meat won't be fall-apart fork-tender.*

Chile Colorado

Starting in the late 1970s, and for about twenty years, my grandparents lived in Albuquerque, New Mexico, where the state question (yes, that's a thing) is "Red or green?" Meaning, which color of chile do you prefer? A work trip in 2000 was the last time I visited the Land of Enchantment, and I vividly recall chowing down on a burrito smothered in red chile sauce. It was almost life-changing. Ever since then, I've sought out both kinds of chile sauces when eating out. Chile colorado has been a favorite of mine at many restaurants—that is, until I figured out how to make a decent sauce at home. And to clear up a misconception I had: The word "colorado" in this instance has nothing to do with the evergreen state—*colorado* in Spanish basically means red (as in blushing). Serve over cauliflower rice (page 30) or a bed of sautéed vegetables, like peppers or cabbage.

—JULIE

SERVES 6 TO 8 / PREP TIME: 15 MINUTES / TOTAL TIME: 4 TO 8 HOURS IN A SLOW COOKER, 45 MINUTES IN A PRESSURE COOKER

FOR THE SAUCE:

3 dried New Mexico chiles

3 dried ancho chiles

1 dried chipotle chile

2 cloves garlic, minced

1 small onion, chopped

3 cups hot water

1 teaspoon dried oregano

1 teaspoon ground cumin

½ teaspoon ground coriander

2 tablespoons olive or coconut oil

3 pounds beef chuck (stew meat works fine) or pork stew meat, cut into bite-size pieces

4 cups chicken or beef stock

To make the sauce:

1. Remove the stems and seeds of the chiles and place them in a large bowl. Add the garlic and onion and cover with the hot water. Allow to soak for 15 minutes. Drain and reserve the soaking liquid.

2. Place the chiles along with the garlic and onion in a food processor or blender. Add the oregano, cumin, and coriander and blend until smooth, adding the reserved soaking liquid as needed to achieve a smooth consistency. Strain through a fine-mesh sieve if you'd like. The sauce can be made up to a week in advance and refrigerated.

Slow cooker method:

1. In a large skillet, heat the oil over medium-high heat. Working in batches, brown the meat. Do not overcrowd the pan.

2. Add the browned meat to a slow cooker, and stir in the chile sauce and stock. Cover and cook on high for 4 to 6 hours or on low for 6 to 8 hours.

Pressure cooker method:

1. Heat a pressure cooker for sautéing (many electric pressure cookers have a sauté feature). Add the oil to the pan and when hot, work in batches to brown the meat, removing to a plate after each batch is done.

2. Return all the meat to the pressure cooker, add the chile sauce and stock. Seal and cook at high pressure for 25 minutes. Use the quick release method to release the pressure.

Stovetop method:

1. In a large Dutch oven, heat the oil over medium-high heat. Working in batches, brown the beef. Return the beef to the pan, add the chile sauce and stock, and bring to a simmer.

2. Cover, and cook over medium-low heat until the beef is fork-tender, about 1 hour.

Kitchen Sink Stew

You are probably going to have those moments when you have a few vegetables that are nearing their peak in your refrigerator. This recipe was born of months of noticing what things we ended up with by week's end. This stew is a great opportunity to make something tasty and clean out the fridge at the same time.

SERVES 6 TO 8 / PREP TIME: 15 MINUTES / TOTAL TIME: 6 TO 8 HOURS IN A SLOW COOKER

2 pounds beef (chuck, roast, stew meat; see Notes), cut into 1-inch cubes

1 teaspoon sea salt

1 teaspoon black pepper

2 tablespoons arrowroot starch/flour

2 tablespoons fat (lard, coconut oil, butter, or ghee)

2 cups diced onion

4 cloves garlic, minced

3 cups beef stock

1 tablespoon coconut aminos

1 tablespoon olive oil

4 cups medium potatoes, peeled and cut into ½-inch cubes

1 leek, white and light green parts, quartered lengthwise

1 cup diced carrots

1 cup sliced mushrooms

1 tablespoon Steak Seasoning (page 223)

1. Season the beef with the salt and pepper, then coat with the arrowroot starch/flour.

2. In a large skillet, heat the fat over medium-high heat. Working in batches, brown the beef. Remove with a slotted spoon and set aside.

3. In the same skillet, sauté the onion and garlic until the onion becomes translucent, 3 to 5 minutes, adding about ½ cup of the stock and the coconut aminos to deglaze the pan as the onions cook.

4. Coat the bottom of a slow cooker (see Notes) with the olive oil and line with potatoes, leek, carrots, and mushrooms. Add the sautéed onions, garlic, beef, and steak seasoning.

5. Pour the remaining stock over everything. Cover and cook on low for 6 to 8 hours.

VARIATIONS: *You can add whatever leftover veggies you have to this. Celery, tomatoes, and peppers are always welcome in this pot. You can also play with the spices. Our household leans toward the spicier side of life.*

NOTES: *If you're using a fattier cut of meat, trim some of the fat off before you brown it.*

  A pressure cooker can be used if you want to eat this meal within an hour. Otherwise, slow and low is the way to go.

Pork Mole

An authentic mole usually has more ingredients than there are pages in this book. However, you can get a mole-like flavor with some relatively accessible ingredients and in a much shorter time frame. Using a slow cooker means almost no hands-on time for you and coming home to a pretty amazing smelling house. Serve hot over cauliflower rice (page 30), Mashed Cauliflower (page 99), or with some Lime Chipotle Slaw (page 94).

SERVES 6 TO 8 / PREP TIME: 10 MINUTES / TOTAL TIME: 6 TO 8 HOURS IN A SLOW COOKER, 25 MINUTES PLUS TIME TO COME TO PRESSURE

1 tablespoon olive or coconut oil

2 pounds pork stew meat

1 cup chopped tomatoes (fresh or canned)

¼ cup pitted dates (or raisins)

2 cloves garlic, minced

½ cup beef or chicken stock

2 tablespoons almond or other nut butter

1 tablespoon unsweetened cocoa powder

2 teaspoons ground cumin

2 teaspoons chili powder

½ teaspoon sea salt

¼ teaspoon black pepper

2 medium sweet potatoes, peeled and cut into ½-inch cubes (about 3 cups)

Slow cooker method:

1. Heat a large skillet over medium-high heat. Add the oil and when shimmering add the pork pieces (working in batches if needed) and brown for a few minutes on each side (see Notes). Add the tomatoes, dates, garlic, stock, almond butter, cocoa, cumin, chili powder, salt, and pepper and stir to incorporate any of the browned bits.

2. Empty the pork and sauce contents into a slow cooker. Cover and cook on low for 6 to 8 hours. About halfway through, add the sweet potatoes to the slow cooker, setting them on top of the meat mixture.

Pressure cooker method:

1. Heat a pressure cooker for sautéing (many electric pressure cookers have a sauté feature). Working in batches, brown the pork in the oil when shimmering for a few minutes on each side (see Notes). Add the tomatoes, dates, garlic, stock, almond butter, cocoa, cumin, chili powder, salt, and pepper, and stir to incorporate any of the browned bits.

2. Place the lid on the pressure cooker and set for 15 minutes at high pressure. Use the quick release method to release the pressure, then add in the sweet potatoes, stir, replace the lid, and cook for 10 more minutes at high pressure.

NOTES: *If you are rushed, skip browning the meat first. It makes a slight taste difference, but not so drastic that you're going to want to avoid this recipe.*

To freeze, combine everything but the sweet potatoes in a resealable freezer bag. When you're ready to cook, simply thaw out the bag contents, place them in the slow cooker, and add the sweet potatoes. Follow the cooking instructions opposite.

VARIATIONS: *We have used kohlrabi and butternut squash instead of sweet potatoes and loved the dish just the same.*

Pork Tinga

Tinga—in a culinary sense—means torn or shredded pieces of meat. Traditionally, in Mexican cooking, anything "tinga" would mean the protein (chicken, beef, pork) in a spicy tomato sauce. This recipe was adapted from Rick Bayless, the popular chef, restaurateur, and author, whose Frontera brand of Mexican-inspired condiments you can probably find at your local grocer. His technique for making the tinga is probably way more authentic than what we do here. He calls for simmering the meat first, cooking white potatoes separately, using another pan to sauté the chorizo, then combining everything at the end. We opt for a simpler approach that still packs a flavor punch but has fewer steps. Oh, and did we mention that if the pork meat is frozen you can still cook it in the pressure cooker? Yep, that's weeknight winning for us!

SERVES 4 TO 6 / PREP TIME: 15 MINUTES / TOTAL TIME: 4 TO 8 HOURS IN A SLOW COOKER, 30 MINUTES IN A PRESSURE COOKER

1 tablespoon olive or coconut oil

½ pound Mexican chorizo (page 68; see Notes)

2 pounds pork stew meat or pork butt (shoulder), cubed

1 yellow or white onion, diced

2 cloves garlic, minced

3 cups chicken stock, store-bought or homemade (page 209)

2 medium sweet potatoes, peeled and cut into cubes

One 28-ounce can diced tomatoes

2 tablespoons adobo sauce from canned chipotles

½ teaspoon dried thyme

4 bay leaves

Slow cooker method:

1. In a large skillet, heat the oil over medium heat. When shimmering, add the chorizo and cook until browned, about 5 minutes. Use a wooden spoon to break up the meat into small bits as it cooks. Transfer to the slow cooker.

2. Add the pork stew meat to the skillet and brown, about 5 minutes. Transfer to the slow cooker.

3. Add the onion, garlic, and a splash of the stock to the skillet, scraping up any browned bits, and cook for a minute more. Add to the slow cooker, along with the remaining stock, sweet potatoes (see Notes), tomatoes, adobo sauce, thyme, and bay leaves.

4. Cover and cook on high for 4 to 6 hours or on low for 6 to 8 hours, until the stew meat is fork tender.

Pressure cooker method:

1. Heat a pressure cooker for sautéing (many electric pressure cookers have a sauté feature). Add the oil and when shimmering, add the chorizo and brown, about 5 minutes, breaking it up with a wooden spoon. Transfer to a plate.

2. Add the pork stew meat and brown for about 5 minutes. Transfer to a plate.

3. Add the onion, garlic, and a splash of the stock to the pan, scraping up any browned bits, and cook for a minute more.

4. Return the chorizo and pork to the pan along with the remaining stock, sweet potatoes (see Notes), tomatoes, chipotle sauce, thyme, and bay leaves. Cover, seal, and cook at high pressure for 20 minutes. Allow pressure to release naturally.

VARIATIONS: *Chicken thighs or beef are also traditional tinga foods and are delicious in this recipe as well. Simply replace the pork stew meat pound-for-pound with the other protein of your choosing. If you'd like to omit the chorizo, that works just as well.*

NOTES: *Sweet potatoes can get very soft in slow cooking and pressure cooking, so if you'd prefer, cook them separately (whatever method you like) and serve them on the side.*

If you are using store-bought Mexican chorizo links, simply remove the casing, then brown as in the instructions above.

Pork Con Thuyen

Nothing screams satisfaction like diving into copious amounts of pork following a twelve-mile obstacle course in the mud. One of our gym members had agreed to do the food and made up a delicious pork banh mi recipe for our crew after completing a Tough Mudder event. His invention got my creative juices flowing a bit. Since *bánh mì* translates to "bread," we had to rename this one, though the flavors and concepts are a bit like what you'd find in those favorite Vietnamese sandwiches. **—CHARLES**

SERVES 6 TO 8 / PREP TIME: 15 MINUTES / TOTAL TIME: 8 HOURS IN A SLOW COOKER

2 to 3 pounds boneless pork butt (shoulder)

1 cup chicken stock, store-bought or homemade (page 209)

¼ cup coconut aminos

2 tablespoons fish sauce

½ teaspoon ground ginger

3 cloves garlic, crushed

6 radishes, julienned or thinly sliced (about ½ cup)

1 large carrot, julienned or thinly sliced

½ cup unseasoned rice vinegar, divided

Juice of 1 lime

1 head romaine or Bibb lettuce

2 cups fresh cilantro, chopped

1 cup pickled sliced jalapeños

1. Place the pork in a slow cooker along with the chicken stock, coconut aminos, fish sauce, ginger, and garlic. Cover and cook on low for 8 hours.

2. Place the radishes and carrots in separate bowls and cover with equal parts of the rice vinegar. Cover and refrigerate until ready to serve.

3. When ready to serve, add the lime juice to the pork and shred with a fork.

4. Spoon the meat into lettuce leaves and garnish with the radish, carrot, cilantro, and jalapeños.

NOTES: *There are a host of kitchen gadgets that can speed up your julienning or slicing. We have peelers, a spiralizer, and a mandoline at the ready.*

Slow Cooker Short Ribs

Short ribs are one of my favorite cuts of meat to eat; they are amazingly aromatic, easy to serve, and make a great dish for company. I prefer an English cut rib, though flanken style works just as well in this recipe. **—CHARLES**

SERVES 3 TO 4 / PREP TIME: 20 MINUTES / TOTAL TIME: 6 TO 8 HOURS IN A SLOW COOKER

3 pounds beef short ribs

Sea salt

1 teaspoon black pepper

2 tablespoons lard

1 cup diced carrots

1 cup diced onion

3 cloves garlic, minced

1 sprig fresh rosemary

1 teaspoon dried thyme

1 bay leaf

2 cups chicken stock, store-bought or homemade (page 209)

1 cup red wine (see Note)

1 tablespoon tomato paste

4 cups cooked cauliflower or yuca root

1. Season the short ribs with 2 teaspoons salt and the pepper. In a large skillet, heat 1 tablespoon of the lard. Working in batches, add the ribs and brown on all sides, 1 to 2 minutes per side. Add them to the slow cooker as they are browned.

2. Add the remaining 1 tablespoon lard to the skillet. Add the carrots, onion, garlic, and a pinch of salt and cook until the onions are soft, about 5 minutes.

3. Add the rosemary, thyme, bay leaf, and chicken stock and stir to deglaze the pan. Add the wine and tomato paste and bring to a quick boil.

4. Remove from the heat and pour the entire mixture over the ribs in the slow cooker. Be sure all the short ribs are covered in liquid. Cover and cook on low for 6 to 8 hours, until the ribs are fork-tender.

5. Using tongs, remove the short ribs from the cooker to a serving tray.

6. Strain out 1 to 2 cups of cooking liquid and puree with the cooked cauliflower or yuca until smooth.

7. Serve the short ribs over the cauliflower or yuca mash with sautéed greens of your choosing.

NOTE: *If you'd rather not use wine, substitute another cup of chicken stock.*

Chicken Verde

Using an Instant Pot means this dish can be on the table in under 30 minutes. We're forever indebted to Michelle Tam (Nom Nom Paleo) for introducing us to the Instant Pot, as it's been a true game changer! Whatever your cooking method of choice (slow cooker, pressure cooker, or stovetop), this recipe is incredibly easy to put together.

SERVES 10 TO 12 / PREP TIME: 5 MINUTES / TOTAL TIME: 2 TO 4 HOURS IN A SLOW COOKER ON HIGH (4 TO 6 HOURS ON LOW), 25 MINUTES IN AN INSTANT POT, 40 MINUTES ON THE STOVETOP

3 pounds boneless, skinless chicken thighs (see Notes)

2 tablespoons chili powder

2 teaspoons ground cumin

2 teaspoons garlic powder

½ teaspoon dried oregano

½ teaspoon onion powder

½ teaspoon sweet paprika

1 teaspoon salt

½ teaspoon black pepper

Two 12- to 14-ounce packages frozen (fire-roasted or not) onions and peppers (see Notes)

2 cups salsa verde, store-bought or homemade (page 219)

Slow cooker method:
1. Place the chicken, chili powder, cumin, garlic powder, oregano, onion powder, paprika, salt, pepper, onions and peppers, and salsa verde in a slow cooker.
2. Cover and cook on high for 2 to 4 hours or on low for 4 to 6 hours.

Pressure cooker method:
1. Place the chicken, chili powder, cumin, garlic powder, oregano, onion powder, paprika, salt, pepper, onions and peppers, and salsa verde in a pressure cooker.
2. Cover, seal, and bring to high pressure, cooking for 15 minutes (or if using an Instant Pot select the poultry function and adjust the time to 15 minutes). Use the quick-release method to vent the pressure cooker, and serve.

Stovetop method:
1. Place the chicken, chili powder, cumin, garlic powder, oregano, onion powder, paprika, salt, pepper, onions and peppers, and salsa verde in a large Dutch oven or soup pot with a lid.
2. Bring to a boil, then reduce the heat to medium-low, and simmer until the chicken is tender and cooked through, about 30 minutes.

NOTES: *While you can brown the chicken first for any of the methods, we didn't find that it made a big taste difference. However, for the Instant Pot method, if you sauté the chicken first, it does speed up how quickly the pot reaches pressure.*

Instead of frozen onions and peppers, you could use 3 bell peppers, sliced, and 1 onion, sliced.

VARIATIONS: *Use a tomato-based salsa instead of a green salsa.*

While the media likes to portray the Paleo diet as a meat-centric way of eating, the reality is that veggies and some fruit usually take up at least half the space on our plates. Many of our main dish recipes include quite a few vegetables, but sometimes we want the vegetables to be the star of the show! These recipes can be side dishes or the main event, depending on your preference and serving size.

Carrot Salad   91
Broccoli Salad   92
Lime Chipotle Slaw   94
Mashed Sweet Potatoes (with Variations)   97
Avocado Salad   98
Mashed Cauliflower (with Variations)   99
Spaghetti Squash Fritters   101
Spanish "Rice"   104
Root Veggie Hash   106
Cauliflower Egg Muffins   107

Carrot Salad

While carrots have never been my favorite vegetable, I find that I like them much more when other people prepare them. I recall a light and fresh parsley and carrot salad my friend Heather made for a lovely al fresco lunch years ago, which I could never quite duplicate. More recently, my sister-in-law, Shada, made this delicious creation when I was visiting family in Philadelphia. According to Shada, this recipe is inspired by the blog *Everybody Likes Sandwiches*, which credits its origination to Dorie Greenspan's recipe in *Around My French Table*.

—JULIE

SERVES 6 TO 8 AS A SIDE DISH / PREP TIME: 10 MINUTES / TOTAL TIME: 15 MINUTES

2 tablespoons Dijon mustard

4 Medjool dates, soaked in ¼ cup hot water and pureed into a paste

¼ cup apple cider vinegar

½ cup olive oil

1 pound carrots, assorted colors, shredded (either with the shredding blade on a food processor or with a box grater)

¼ cup chopped Italian (flat-leaf) parsley

3 tablespoons slivered almonds

2 green onions, thinly sliced

1. In a small bowl, stir together the mustard, date paste, and cider vinegar. Whisk in the olive oil. (You can also combine in a small food processor.)

2. In a large bowl, combine the carrots, parsley, almonds, and green onions. Add the dressing and toss. Serve chilled (see Note).

NOTE: *This salad holds up well as leftovers and travels well for potlucks and picnics.*

VARIATION: *Currants or raisins add an additional sweet kick.*

Broccoli Salad

Typically oozing with lots of mayonnaise and a hefty amount of sugar, the average broccoli salad isn't the most suitable for a healthy diet. Here we change up the flavors a bit, but still hold true to that bacon tradition. Why mess with a good thing?

SERVES 6 TO 8 / PREP TIME: 10 MINUTES / TOTAL TIME: 10 MINUTES

1 bunch broccoli, cut into small florets

½ cup raisins

¼ cup sunflower seeds

¼ cup finely minced red onion

¼ cup chopped pecans (optional)

½ cup mayonnaise, store-bought or homemade (page 211)

¼ cup red wine vinegar or apple cider vinegar

5 slices bacon, cooked until crispy and chopped, bacon drippings reserved

Salt and black pepper

1. In a large bowl, mix together the broccoli, raisins, sunflower seeds, onion, and pecans (if using).

2. In a separate bowl, whisk together the mayo, vinegar, and reserved bacon drippings.

3. Pour the dressing over the broccoli and mix in the bacon. Season with salt and pepper to taste. Refrigerate until ready to serve.

VARIATION: *You can easily convert this into an Asian-style salad by making a few changes: Swap out the red onion for 3 or 4 thinly sliced green onions. Omit the bacon. Substitute 2 tablespoons sesame seeds for the sunflower seeds. For the dressing, use rice vinegar instead of red wine vinegar and add 2 teaspoons sesame oil along with the mayo.*

Lime Chipotle Slaw

The last time I was in Philadelphia my family took us out to Fette Sau (which is German for "fat pig"). Though the north isn't known for its barbecue and slaw, Fette Sau might be changing that notion. The brisket and wings were outstanding, yet I found my favorite item on the menu was the slaw that accompanied my meal. I wish I'd had the gumption to go up and ask a member of the kitchen team what was in the slaw, but in the moment my head and mouth were too busy to do anything but savor the flavors. This is my best guess at what was in the dish, as admittedly that whole trip is a bit of a blur given that it involved about thirty-two hours of car time (1,600 miles), two children in diapers, and one grown-up. But I do remember the slaw. . . .

—JULIE

SERVES 6 TO 8 / PREP TIME: 10 MINUTES / TOTAL TIME: 10 MINUTES

1 head red or green cabbage or a mix of both, shredded

2 to 3 jalapeño peppers, seeded and sliced into long pieces

2 carrots, shredded (optional)

¼ cup fresh lime juice (about 2 limes)

¼ cup chopped fresh cilantro

1 tablespoon adobo sauce from canned chipotles

½ teaspoon ground cumin

½ cup mayonnaise, store-bought or homemade (page 211)

Salt and black pepper

1. In a large bowl, combine the cabbage, jalapeños, and carrots (if using).

2. Meanwhile, in a small food processor or blender, combine the lime juice, cilantro, adobo sauce, cumin, and mayo. Taste and season with salt and black pepper to taste.

3. Pour the dressing over the cabbage and mix well (hands are always appropriate mixing utensils). Keep refrigerated until ready to serve.

VARIATIONS: *Go on and get crazy with adding in other vegetables that appeal to you. Some thinly sliced bell peppers, jicama, other kinds of cabbage, and sliced red onions are all great additions to this slaw! Add more chipotle sauce for even more kick.*

Mashed Sweet Potatoes (with Variations)

A perennial favorite in Paleo circles, mashed sweet potatoes are a perfect side dish for just about anything. These potatoes are sweet all on their own, so adding extra sweetener really is not necessary, but a tiny bit of maple syrup (with the bacon pecan variation) is a nice touch if you want.

SERVES 4 TO 6 / PREP TIME: 10 MINUTES / TOTAL TIME: 25 MINUTES

2 pounds sweet potatoes, peeled and cubed (see Note)

About 2 tablespoons coconut milk or heavy cream, plus more as needed

2 tablespoons fat (ghee, butter, or coconut butter)

½ teaspoon salt

1. Place the sweet potatoes in a large pan and cover with water. Bring to a boil over high heat and cook until the potatoes are fork-tender, about 15 minutes. Drain and return to the pot. (Alternatively, you can steam in a steamer basket for about 15 minutes.)

2. Add the coconut milk, fat, and salt to the hot sweet potatoes and use a hand mixer, immersion blender, or potato masher to mash. Add more liquid to achieve your desired consistency.

Mashed Chipotle Lime Sweet Potatoes: After making the mash, add 1 tablespoon (or less if you don't want it too spicy) chipotle sauce (page 227) or adobo sauce from canned chipotles in adobo, and the juice and grated zest of 1 lime.

Mashed Bacon Pecan Sweet Potatoes: After making the mash, add 4 slices cooked and crumbled bacon and ¼ cup chopped toasted pecans.

NOTE: *While some stores and markets use "yam" and "sweet potato" interchangeably, chances are you'll be buying some variation of a sweet potato. Quite large with a thick brown skin, true yams are native to Africa and Asia and are not usually carried in your local grocery store.*

Avocado Salad

With lots of healthy fats thanks to the avocado and olive oil, this salad is quite filling and perfect for the dog days of summer. Top with some seared steak, grilled chicken, or fish to make it a complete meal.

SERVES 4 / PREP TIME: 10 MINUTES / TOTAL TIME: 10 MINUTES

2 cloves garlic, minced

¼ cup red wine vinegar

1 teaspoon dried oregano

Juice of 1 lemon

½ teaspoon sea salt

¼ teaspoon black pepper

½ cup extra-virgin olive oil

2 large Hass avocados, pitted, peeled, and diced

¾ cup kalamata olives, pitted and halved

¾ cup green olives, pitted and halved

1 cup grape or cherry tomatoes, halved

¼ cup fresh cilantro leaves, chopped

1. In a medium bowl, whisk together the garlic, red wine vinegar, oregano, lemon juice, salt, and pepper. Whisk in the olive oil to combine well. (You can also make this in a small food processor or small blender.)

2. In a large bowl, combine the avocados, olives, tomatoes, and cilantro. Pour in about two-thirds of the dressing. Taste and add the remaining dressing if needed.

Mashed Cauliflower (with Variations)

Cauliflower is pretty much the vegetable darling in Paleo and low-carb circles. Why? It can be an alternative to rice or mashed potatoes, it can make soups and casseroles "creamy," it's delicious oven-roasted, and it provides a great dose of vitamin C, dietary fiber, B vitamins, and other nutrients. Our secret to flavorful mashed cauliflower? Cook the cauliflower in chicken stock (or broth). Of course, finishing off your mash with a dollop of butter doesn't hurt either!

MAKES ABOUT 4 CUPS / PREP TIME: 5 MINUTES / TOTAL TIME: 20 MINUTES

1 medium head cauliflower, stem removed, coarsely chopped into florets

1 cup chicken stock

1 clove garlic, smashed

1 sprig fresh rosemary

1 to 2 tablespoons butter, ghee, or coconut butter (optional)

Mix-ins (optional; see Variations)

1. In a large saucepan or Dutch oven, combine the cauliflower, stock, garlic, and rosemary and bring to a boil.
2. Reduce the heat to medium, cover, and cook until the cauliflower is very tender and easily mashed with a fork, 15 to 20 minutes. You may need to add more stock if you run out of liquid and the cauliflower is not yet cooked through. If there is stock that remains, drain it off and set aside.
3. Pour the cooked cauliflower into a food processor and puree until smooth. If the cauliflower seems too dry, add some of the reserved stock.
4. Add the butter (if using) and any optional mix-ins.

Mashed Sun-Dried Tomato and Basil Cauliflower: After making the mash, stir in ¼ to ½ cup chopped (reconstituted) sun-dried tomatoes and ¼ cup fresh basil (chiffonade or mince is fine).

Southwestern Mashed Cauliflower: After making the mash, mix in 2 teaspoons adobo sauce (from canned chipotles), ½ teaspoon ground cumin, and ½ teaspoon grated lime zest along with the juice of 1 lime.

Mashed Cheddar and Bacon Cauliflower: After making the mash, stir in ½ cup shredded cheddar cheese (if you eat dairy) and ¼ cup bacon crumbles.

Spaghetti Squash Fritters

This recipe is inspired by one in Mollie Katzen's book *The Vegetable Dishes I Can't Live Without*.

Heads up! This recipe calls for already cooked spaghetti squash. See "How to Cook Spaghetti Squash" (page 102) for instructions. **—JULIE**

MAKES ABOUT 1 DOZEN FRITTERS / PREP TIME: 10 MINUTES (NOT COUNTING TIME TO COOK SPAGHETTI SQUASH) / TOTAL TIME: 25 MINUTES

3 cups cooked spaghetti squash, strands separated (from 1 large squash)

⅓ cup arrowroot starch/flour

½ teaspoon salt

1 green onion, sliced

4 slices bacon, cooked and crumbled

3 large eggs

1 to 2 tablespoons coconut oil or cooking fat of your choice

1. Place the squash in a large bowl. If it's too moist, wrap it in some paper towels and squeeze out the excess liquid.
2. Add the arrowroot starch/flour, salt, green onion, and bacon and stir to combine well.
3. Whisk the eggs in a small bowl, then add them to the squash mixture and stir to combine.
4. Heat a large skillet over medium heat. Add enough oil to coat the pan, and when it's hot, spoon the squash mixture to form fritters of your desired size; ¼ cup per fritter works well.
5. When the fritters are crispy and browned on one side, about 5 minutes, use a spatula to flip them and continue cooking on the other side until crisped, about 5 minutes longer. Serve hot.

VARIATIONS: *Make it a meal! Mix some already cooked chicken into the fritters and you essentially have a one-dish supper.*

We also love to add about 1 tablespoon hot sauce to the mixture for Buffalo-style fritters.

HOW TO COOK SPAGHETTI SQUASH

FOR ELECTRIC PRESSURE COOKING: Halve the squash crosswise and remove the seeds. Place the squash halves into a steamer basket in the pressure cooker pot, cut side down. Add 1 cup water to the pressure cooker pot. Set pressure cooker time for 7 minutes at high pressure. Use the quick pressure release. Carefully remove the squash and when cool, scrape out the spaghetti strands.

FOR OVEN-BAKING: Preheat the oven to 400°F. Halve the squash crosswise. (We used to recommend lengthwise, but a few near misses later, and thanks to the wise Michelle Tam, aka Nom Nom Paleo, we now only prepare ours cutting crosswise—it's so much easier to cut, plus the strands come out much longer this way.) Remove the seeds. Place the squash halves cut side down in a baking pan or on a baking sheet. Bake until a fork can easily pierce the flesh, 30 to 45 minutes. We typically cook ours a bit on the al dente side, which is on the lower end of the cooking time—especially if the squash is going to be used in another recipe like the Spaghetti Squash Fritters on page 101. Scrape out the spaghetti "strands" to use in your favorite recipe.

TO MICROWAVE: Halve the squash crosswise and remove the seeds. Place the squash halves cut side down in a microwave-safe baking dish (like a 9 x 13-inch Pyrex pan). Add about ½ inch water to the pan, place in the microwave, and cook on high for 10 to 15 minutes, or until squash is cooked al dente. Carefully remove the pan from the microwave and scrape out the strands.

HOW TO MAKE CAST IRON NONSTICK

We used to shy away from the cast-iron pan because of cleaning and sticking issues. Now? Either we've gotten ours so well seasoned from cooking so much bacon, or we've just gotten better at using it. We like to think the latter. What have we learned along the way? For starters, always heat up the pan to a pretty high heat! Yep, even for scrambled eggs. When hot, add a generous amount of fat (ghee, butter, tallow, lard, coconut oil, avocado oil, etc.). A properly heated pan makes all the difference when it comes to things not sticking, and a decent amount of fat is super important too!

Spanish "Rice"

Is this truly Spanish or is it Mexican rice? Some say true Spanish rice involves saffron, and Mexican rice includes chiles and peppers. We don't really know which is correct—what we do know is that this is a great side dish for our Green Enchiladas (page 36) or meatballs made with Southwestern meat mix (page 55). If you want to make this vegetarian, use vegetable stock instead of chicken stock.

SERVES 6 TO 8 / PREP TIME: 15 MINUTES / TOTAL TIME: 30 MINUTES

One 14-ounce can whole or diced tomatoes (about 2 cups)

1 medium yellow onion, minced

1 tablespoon fat (coconut oil, olive oil, bacon grease, etc.)

2 ribs celery, minced

1 green bell pepper, diced

1 medium head cauliflower, riced (see "How to Make Cauliflower Rice," page 30), about 6 cups

2 garlic cloves, minced

½ cup chicken stock, store-bought or homemade (page 209)

2 teaspoons ground cumin

½ teaspoon cayenne pepper

⅓ cup chopped fresh cilantro leaves (optional)

Salt and black pepper

1. In a food processor or blender, puree the tomatoes and onion until smooth.

2. Heat a large, deep skillet or Dutch oven over medium-high heat and add the fat. When shimmering, stir in the celery and bell pepper. Sauté until the vegetables have softened, 3 to 5 minutes.

3. Stir in the riced cauliflower and cook until browned, 3 to 4 minutes. Stir in the garlic and sauté for a minute more.

4. Stir in the tomato-onion puree, the stock, cumin, and cayenne and bring to a simmer. Cover and cook until most of the liquid has evaporated, about 10 minutes. Stir in the cilantro (if using), and season with salt and black pepper to taste.

VARIATIONS: *Olives, jalapeño or poblano peppers, or even carrots are all great additions to this dish. Play around with what works for you.*

Root Veggie Hash

Parcooking root vegetables helps reduce the amount of time they need to cook on the stove or in the oven. We use a microwave in this recipe. If you choose not to use microwaves, you can boil or steam the vegetables on the stovetop. You'll see that the parcooking is truly optional—cooking entirely on the stovetop just adds a bit of time to total preparation.

SERVES 6 TO 8 / PREP TIME: 15 MINUTES / TOTAL TIME: 30 MINUTES

1 large sweet potato, peeled and cut into ½-inch cubes

3 medium carrots, peeled and cut into ½-inch cubes

1 medium parsnip, peeled and cut into ½-inch cubes

1 turnip, peeled and cut into ½-inch cubes

2 tablespoons fat (coconut oil, lard, or other fat of choice)

2 cloves garlic, minced

¾ teaspoon salt

1 tablespoon fresh rosemary, minced

1. To parcook (optional): Place the sweet potato, carrots, parsnip, and turnip in a large microwave-safe bowl and cover with water. Cook on high until the vegetables are just barely soft, 6 to 8 minutes. Drain in a colander.

2. Heat a large cast-iron or stainless steel skillet over medium-high heat. Add the fat and when shimmering, add the vegetables. Allow to cook, without stirring, until starting to brown, about 5 minutes. Stir and continue to cook until the veggies are softened, about 5 to 10 minutes, or longer if not parcooked.

3. Stir in the garlic, salt, and rosemary. Cook for 2 minutes more. Serve hot (see Note).

NOTE: *Any leftover hash is a great breakfast side dish.*

VARIATION: *Beets, rutabagas, and white potatoes also work well in this recipe.*

Cauliflower Egg Muffins

True story: I once tried to make a cheesy cauliflower pizza crust. This was back before we transitioned to a full-Paleo way of eating. While the flavor was decent (thank you, cheese!) it was rather soggy and not conducive to holding a nice slice in your hand. I decided then and there to quit trying to use cauliflower for pizza crust, but I didn't give up on it in all sorts of other preparations—like as a base for these muffins. Here's the nifty thing about these muffins: They're a loose template, subject to whatever mix-ins you choose (though we're happy to suggest a few of our favorites). This is a great way to get extra vegetables into the kiddos—and ourselves—while also packing a decent protein punch. Oh, and another added bonus, these are super portable.

—JULIE

MAKES 12 MUFFINS / PREP TIME: 10 MINUTES / TOTAL TIME: 30 MINUTES

Fat (butter, coconut oil, or other oil), for the muffin tin

4 large eggs

4 cups (about ½ large head) riced cauliflower (see "How to Make Cauliflower Rice, page 30)

1 teaspoon sea salt

½ teaspoon black pepper

Mix-in of your choice (see Note)

1. Preheat the oven to 400°F. Liberally grease 12 cups of a muffin tin with the fat of your choosing.

2. In a large bowl, whisk the eggs. Stir in the cauliflower, salt, pepper, and your desired mix-in.

3. Divide the mixture among the 12 muffin cups, pressing down slightly to remove any air pockets.

4. Bake until the eggs are cooked through, about 20 minutes. Allow to cool in the pan before removing.

SUGGESTED MIX-INS

½ cup diced ham + ½ cup diced bell peppers

4 slices cooked, crumbled bacon + ½ cup coarsely chopped cooked broccoli

1 cup chopped cooked chicken + 3 tablespoons hot sauce

½ cup cooked ground beef + 2 tablespoons tomato paste + 1 teaspoon dried oregano

1 cup chopped fully cooked sausage + ½ cup diced mushrooms + ½ cup baby spinach

VARIATION: *If you tolerate and use dairy, try topping any of these with a favorite cheese before you bake them.*

ONE-DISH MEALS

Simple one-dish meals mean less prep and less cleanup, which means more time for sitting down and enjoying a nice meal with friends or family.

Chicken Cacciatore   111
Meat and Sweet Potato Skillet   112
Creamy Shrimp with Vegetables   115
One-Pan Roast Salmon and Asparagus   116
Pork Medallions with Balsamic Mustard   117
Crispy Chicken with Peppery Pesto Pasta   118
One-Pan Fajitas   120
Lamb and Rice Stew   123
Roast Chicken Thighs with Veggies   124
Oven-Roasted Steaks with Broccoli and Cauliflower   127
Turkey with Mushrooms and Green Beans   128
Skillet Steaks with Veggies and Potatoes   130
Turkey Cutlets with Stuffing   132
Turkey or Chicken Pesto Pasta Bake   135
Shrimp and Okra Skillet   137
Basil-Ginger Pork   138

Chicken Cacciatore

When I was growing up, my family's version of Italian food typically involved spaghetti sauce from a jar or canned ravioli—you know the ones. However, we did get a wee bit more authentic when it came to a few dishes, like Grandpa's lasagna and chicken cacciatore. I can still envision the pan on the stove, with the chicken legs and thighs swimming in a bubbling tomato sauce. The great thing about this is that you can use any chicken parts, and it's even great in the slow cooker.

—JULIE

SERVES 4 TO 6 / PREP TIME: 10 MINUTES / TOTAL TIME: 40 MINUTES

2 to 3 pounds bone-in, skin-on chicken legs and thighs (or any chicken parts of your choosing; see Notes)

1 teaspoon salt

½ teaspoon black pepper

2 tablespoons olive oil or other cooking fat

1 medium onion, sliced

4 cloves garlic, minced

12 ounces white mushrooms, sliced

2 green bell peppers, seeded and sliced

1 cup pitted kalamata olives

1 teaspoon dried oregano

One 28-ounce can whole or diced tomatoes (I prefer San Marzano)

1 cup chicken stock, store-bought or homemade (page 209)

1. Pat the chicken pieces dry and season with the salt and black pepper.

2. Heat a large Dutch oven or deep skillet with a lid over medium-high heat. When hot, add the oil, and when shimmering, add the chicken parts, skin side down.

3. Working in batches if necessary, brown the chicken for 3 to 4 minutes per side and transfer to a plate (you aren't cooking the chicken all the way through, just browning the exterior).

4. Reduce the heat to medium. Add the onion, garlic, mushrooms, and bell peppers to the pan and stir to loosen up any of the browned bits. Cook until the vegetables have softened, 5 to 6 minutes.

5. Stir in the olives, oregano, tomatoes, and chicken stock. Return the chicken to the pan skin side up, increase the heat to high, and bring the sauce to a boil. Reduce the heat to medium-low, cover, and cook until chicken is cooked through, 25 to 35 minutes.

NOTES: *To make this faster, use boneless, skinless chicken breasts or thighs, and reduce the cooking time in step 5 to only 10 to 15 minutes. If you prefer a thicker sauce, after the chicken is cooked through, transfer it to a platter and cover to keep warm, then simmer the sauce over medium-low heat to reduce.*

Meat and Sweet Potato Skillet

We labeled this one "meat" and sweet potato skillet because sometimes we use ground venison, sometimes we use beef, sometimes we use lamb . . . it just depends. This one-skillet dish takes the meat of your choosing, a bunch of flavorful spices, and makes for great comfort food. If you feel a need for some green veggies to go with this, try our Broccoli Salad (page 92) or a simple sauté of spinach with garlic.

SERVES 6 TO 8 / PREP TIME: 10 MINUTES / TOTAL TIME: 25 MINUTES

2 tablespoons coconut oil

2 medium sweet potatoes, peeled and diced

3 cloves garlic, minced

1 medium onion, diced

2 pounds ground meat (beef, venison, turkey, chicken, or pork)

1 teaspoon smoked paprika

1 teaspoon dried oregano

1 teaspoon ground cumin

1 teaspoon salt

½ teaspoon black pepper

1. Heat a large skillet over medium heat. Add 1 tablespoon of the coconut oil and once hot, add the sweet potatoes, garlic, and onion and brown the potatoes on all sides until they begin to soften, about 8 minutes. Remove to a plate.

2. Add the remaining 1 tablespoon oil to the skillet. Add the meat and cook until browned and cooked through. Use a wooden spoon to break up the meat into small bits as it cooks.

3. Once the meat is cooked, return the sweet potatoes to the skillet and stir in the paprika, oregano, cumin, salt, and pepper. Taste and adjust the seasoning to your preference.

VARIATIONS: *Try some parsnips, diced butternut squash, kohlrabi, or any variety of sweet potatoes.*

Creamy Shrimp with Vegetables

Even though this is a creamy dish, the fact that it involves zucchini, shrimp, spinach, and lemon makes for a surprisingly light—but filling—one-dish supper. Don't have shrimp or don't like crustaceans? Opt for chicken or scallops instead.

SERVES 3 TO 4 / PREP TIME: 10 MINUTES / TOTAL TIME: 20 MINUTES

2 tablespoons fat (ghee, butter, or coconut oil)

2 leeks, white and light green parts, halved lengthwise then sliced crosswise

1 clove garlic, minced

1 pound peeled and deveined shrimp

Grated zest of 1 lemon

2 medium zucchini, halved lengthwise and then sliced crosswise into half-moons

¼ cup chicken stock, store-bought or homemade (page 209)

½ cup heavy cream or full-fat coconut milk

8 cups spinach

Salt and black pepper

1. Heat a large skillet over medium heat. Add the fat and when hot, add the leeks and sauté until the leeks are softened, 3 to 5 minutes. Add the garlic and sauté a minute more.

2. Add the shrimp and lemon zest and cook until the shrimp are pink and mostly cooked, about 4 minutes.

3. Stir in the zucchini, stock, cream, and spinach. Cover and cook, stirring a few times, until the spinach has cooked down, about 5 minutes. Season with salt and pepper to taste.

VARIATION: *Mix in some ginger and mushrooms and omit the lemon zest, and this dish comes close to a Chinese stir-fry dish.*

One-Pan Roast Salmon and Asparagus

You may have picked up on the fact that we are huge fans of the put-a-bunch-of-stuff-in-a-pot-or-pan-and-that's-dinner approach. Fish—since it cooks so quickly—makes for some of the quickest dinners out there, but you have to be cautious about what you cook it with and for how long. This one is perfect for spring when asparagus is in season at the farmers' market. Feel free to swap the salmon for cod, halibut, or arctic char, and/or the asparagus for fresh green beans or artichoke hearts (frozen or canned in water). If you're not a fan of capers, try some of the sauces listed on pages 157 to 160 instead.

SERVES 3 TO 4 / PREP TIME: 10 MINUTES / TOTAL TIME: 20 MINUTES

2 tablespoons olive oil

1 pound skin-on salmon fillet, cut into 4 even portions

1 lemon, sliced into rounds

1 pound asparagus, tough ends removed

3 tablespoons ghee, butter, or other fat

3 tablespoons capers, rinsed

1 clove garlic, minced

1 tablespoon fresh lemon juice

1 tablespoon minced Italian (flat-leaf) parsley

Salt and black pepper

1. Preheat the oven to 425°F. Line a rimmed baking sheet with foil (this makes cleanup a breeze) and drizzle with a little bit of the oil.

2. Place the salmon pieces skin-side down in the middle of the pan and top with 1 or 2 lemon rounds apiece. Place the asparagus around the salmon, drizzle with the remaining olive oil, and stir to coat.

3. Bake until the salmon is just beginning to flake easily, about 10 minutes.

4. Meanwhile, melt the ghee in a microwave-safe bowl (or on the stovetop in a saucepan). Once melted, stir in the capers, garlic, and lemon juice.

5. Spoon the sauce over the salmon and asparagus, then sprinkle with the parsley and salt and pepper to taste.

Pork Medallions with Balsamic Mustard

Pork tenderloin makes for a super-quick protein choice. Note that there is a difference between pork loin and pork tenderloin. Tenderloins are typically long, relatively thin pieces of meat that are lean and quick cooking, whereas loins are much thicker, usually fattier, and lend themselves well to long, slow methods of cooking like stewing.

SERVES 3 TO 4 / PREP TIME: 10 MINUTES / TOTAL TIME: 40 TO 45 MINUTES

1 pound pork tenderloin, trimmed of any silver skin, cut crosswise into medallions about 1 inch thick

¾ teaspoon salt

¼ teaspoon plus a dash black pepper

1 tablespoon fat (coconut oil, lard, olive oil, or other fat of choice)

2 cups peeled and cubed (½ inch) butternut squash

2 tablespoons olive oil or avocado oil

2 tablespoons balsamic vinegar

1 tablespoon Dijon mustard

1 tablespoon fresh rosemary, minced

1 medium red or yellow onion, sliced

2 cups whole mushrooms (white button, baby bellas, or cremini), wiped clean, tough stems removed, then sliced

1 tablespoon chopped fresh Italian (flat-leaf) parsley

1. Preheat the oven to 425°F.

2. Heat a large ovenproof skillet over medium-high heat. While the pan is heating, season the pork medallions with ¼ teaspoon each of the salt and pepper. When the pan is hot, add the fat, and when shimmering, add the pork to the pan. Cook until just browned, about 2 minutes per side. Remove to a plate and set aside—the pork will not be cooked through at this point.

3. Add the butternut squash to the pan and brown for 2 to 3 minutes.

4. Meanwhile, in a small bowl, whisk together the oil, vinegar, mustard, and rosemary and set aside.

5. Remove the pan from the heat. Add the onion and mushrooms to the pan, and pour the vinegar mixture over all. Stir to combine.

6. Place the pan in the oven and bake until the squash is almost softened, about 10 minutes.

7. Put the pork medallions on top of the vegetables and finish in the oven until an instant-read thermometer inserted in the pork registers 145°F, about 10 to 15 minutes. Sprinkle the parsley over the pork and vegetables.

Crispy Chicken with Peppery Pesto Pasta

A one-dish wonder with some crispy chicken to boot. We highly recommend using a splatter screen for this one, as the time it takes to clean the kitchen is very often our biggest reason to want to skip out on cooking!

SERVES 6 TO 8 / PREP TIME: 10 MINUTES / TOTAL TIME: 35 TO 40 MINUTES

3 pounds bone-in or boneless, skin-on chicken thighs

1 teaspoon salt

1 teaspoon black pepper

2 teaspoons seasoning (we use Penzeys Berbere Seasoning, paprika, or anything else)

2 teaspoons fat (coconut oil, lard, tallow, or ghee)

FOR THE PESTO AND ZUCCHINI

1 cup firmly packed arugula

¼ cup Italian (flat-leaf) parsley

¼ cup fresh cilantro

¼ cup olive oil

1 clove garlic, crushed

2 teaspoons fresh lemon juice

½ teaspoon salt

½ teaspoon black pepper

¼ cup walnuts (optional)

3 zucchini, julienned or spiralized into pasta-like noodles (page 67)

1. Pat the chicken thighs dry. Sprinkle the skin side with some of the salt and pepper. Flip over and season the meat side with the remaining salt and pepper and whatever seasoning you choose.

2. Preheat the oven to 400°F.

3. Heat a large ovenproof cast-iron or stainless steel skillet over high heat. Add the fat and when hot, add the chicken thighs, skin side down. Reduce the heat to medium-high and cook the thighs for 10 minutes, until the skin is crispy and browned (the chicken pieces will give off a lot of juices, causing quite a lot of splatter. Now is a perfect time to use a splatter screen!). Turn the pieces over and cook for a few minutes on the skinless side, just until slightly browned. Remove the chicken to a plate.

4. Meanwhile, make the pesto: In a food processor, combine the arugula, parsley, cilantro, oil, garlic, lemon juice, salt, pepper, and walnuts (if using) and process until well combined.

5. In the pan the chicken was cooked in, toss the zucchini noodles with pesto (see Note).

6. Place the chicken pieces on top of the zucchini, skin side up, and place the entire pan in the oven. Bake until the chicken pieces are cooked through, 10 to 15 minutes.

NOTE: *If you prefer raw noodles to cooked, in step 5 simply toss the noodles with the pesto in a separate bowl and cook the chicken in the oven until cooked through.*

One-Pan Fajitas

Our favorite local Mexican restaurant has what they call the "Santa Lucia Special" for two. It's essentially a stir-fry plate with shrimp, chicken, beef, peppers, and onions. The servers always look at us a bit strangely when we request "no rice, no beans, no sour cream," and "extra veggies in the fajitas," but we're kind of used to that. This recipe enables us to chow down on one of our favorites at home without modifications—and no tipping required.

SERVES 6 TO 8 / PREP TIME: 5 TO 10 MINUTES / TOTAL TIME: 20 TO 30 MINUTES

2 pounds meat (flank or skirt steak, chicken breasts or thighs), cut into strips

3 tablespoons fajita or taco seasoning, store-bought or homemade (page 224)

¼ cup oil (olive, avocado, or melted coconut oil)

Two 14-ounce packages frozen fire-roasted peppers and onions (see Notes)

1 lime, halved

1. Preheat a large skillet, preferably cast iron, over high heat (see Notes).

2. While the pan is heating (you want it super hot), place your meat of choice in a medium bowl and toss with the fajita seasoning and the oil.

3. Add half the meat mixture to the hot pan and cook for 2 to 3 minutes (without stirring), then stir and cook a minute or two longer or until just undercooked. Remove the meat to a clean plate and repeat with the remaining meat.

4. When the second batch of meat is almost cooked through, add the first batch back to the pan along with the peppers and onions. Squeeze the lime juice over the pan and stir, cooking until the peppers and onions are just softened with a slightly browned edge, about 7 minutes.

NOTES: *If you prefer, you can cook the whole enchilada (well, here we mean fajitas) on baking sheets all at once—no stovetop required. Simply preheat your oven to 400°F and place two baking sheets in the oven as you preheat. Toss the meat and veggies with the seasonings and oil in a large bowl. Divide evenly between the two pans and cook until cooked through, 20 to 25 minutes.*

Instead of frozen peppers and onions you can slice 3 bell peppers and 1 onion.

VARIATION: *One restaurant we've been to adds cauliflower, broccoli, mushrooms, and zucchini to their fajitas. We can't disagree with more veggies and think it's awesome to have so many other vegetables added!*

Lamb and Rice Stew

One-pot meals are always welcome in our busy household. They make for perfect leftovers and freeze well too. We always try to keep some kind of soup or stew on hand in the refrigerator or freezer, and this is one of our favorites.

SERVES 3 TO 4 / PREP TIME: 10 MINUTES / TOTAL TIME: 1 HOUR

½ cup slivered almonds

2 tablespoons coconut oil

1 cup finely chopped red onion

1 cup finely chopped carrot

½ cup finely chopped celery

1 pound lamb shoulder, cut into ½-inch chunks

½ teaspoon ground cumin

¼ teaspoon ground cinnamon

¼ teaspoon ground nutmeg

One 14-ounce can crushed tomatoes

1 head cauliflower, riced (see "How to Make Cauliflower Rice," page 30)

1 cup vegetable stock

¼ cup finely chopped chives

¼ cup finely chopped fresh cilantro

Grated zest of 1 orange

Orange slices, for garnish

1. Preheat the oven to 300°F.

2. In a large Dutch oven, combine the almonds and coconut oil and toast the almonds over medium heat, about 1 minute.

3. Add the onion, carrot, and celery and cook until they begin to soften, 4 to 6 minutes. Increase the heat to medium-high, add the lamb, and cook for 5 to 6 minutes to brown.

4. Sprinkle the cumin, cinnamon, and nutmeg over the meat and stir in, then add the tomatoes. Stir in the riced cauliflower and stock.

5. Cover and place in the oven. Bake for 30 minutes.

6. Remove from the oven, uncover, and let sit for 5 minutes. Stir in the chives, cilantro, and orange zest. Garnish with thinly sliced orange and serve.

Roast Chicken Thighs with Veggies

A few years back, we were commenting with friends about how awesome chicken schmaltz is, bewildered that anyone would throw away delicious chicken fat. We took it upon ourselves to roast some yuca fries in the lovely and flavorful chicken fat along with pan drippings from the meat, which then led us to roasting a whole variety of vegetables in the drippings. Waste not, want not, right? This recipe harnesses that goodness into one pan all while adding great flavor to the vegetables. Plus, it cooks quite quickly compared to a roasting a whole chicken (see page 26).

SERVES 6 TO 8 / PREP TIME: 10 MINUTES / TOTAL TIME: 40 MINUTES

3 pounds bone-in, skin-on chicken thighs, patted dry

1 pound Brussels sprouts, trimmed and halved

1 pound carrots, assorted colors, cut into ½- to 1-inch pieces

1 pound sweet potatoes, peeled and cut into ½-inch cubes

3 shallots, peeled, root end trimmed off, and quartered

3 cloves garlic, minced

2 tablespoons olive oil

1 tablespoon minced fresh rosemary (or 1 teaspoon dried)

2 teaspoons minced fresh thyme (or ¾ teaspoon dried)

2 teaspoons salt

1. Preheat the oven to 475°F.

2. Place the chicken thighs on a rimmed baking sheet skin side up. Scatter the vegetables, shallots, and garlic around the chicken.

3. Drizzle the olive oil over everything, making sure the vegetables are well coated. Sprinkle the rosemary, thyme, and salt over the chicken and vegetables.

4. Place the pan in the oven and bake for 30 to 40 minutes, stirring the vegetables about halfway through cooking. Chicken should be cooked through (internal temperature of 165°F). If you like your chicken skin extra crispy, put the pan under the broiler set to high for about 5 minutes.

VARIATIONS: *Any heartier vegetables (butternut squash, parsnips, etc.) would work well with this dish, though we happen to love the ones here. You could use faster-cooking ones like broccoli or cauliflower or even summer squash—but wait to add them until the chicken is about halfway cooked. We like our veggies crispy and browned, so keep that in mind.*

Pork chops would also work fine here—the cooking time may increase somewhat depending on thickness, and unless you choose particularly fatty chops, you won't have as much drippings to bathe your vegetables in.

Oven-Roasted Steaks with Broccoli and Cauliflower

Using one pan for cooking makes for easy cleanup and ensures that all those drippings from the steak don't go to waste!

SERVES 4 TO 6 / PREP TIME: 10 MINUTES / TOTAL TIME: 30 MINUTES

Two 10-ounce steaks, cut of your choice

Salt and black pepper

1 pound broccoli, cut into small florets

1 pound cauliflower, cut into small florets (see Note)

1 small onion, sliced

2 tablespoons olive oil

5 cloves garlic, minced

1. Position the rack about 4 inches away from the heating element and preheat the broiler to high. Place a wire rack on a rimmed baking sheet.

2. Liberally season the steaks with salt and pepper. Place on the wire rack and then put them in the oven. Broil until the first sides are browned but not burned, about 3 minutes. Flip over the steaks, and broil until the other sides are browned, about 3 minutes longer (the steak should still be very much on the rare side at this point). Remove from the oven and let sit on the rack in the pan for a few minutes. Turn off the broiler and set the oven to 475°F.

3. In a large bowl, combine the vegetables, olive oil, and garlic and toss to coat. Remove the wire rack and steaks from the baking sheet.

4. Pour the vegetables onto the sheet and mix with any of the drippings from the steaks. Place the vegetables in the oven and roast for 10 minutes, stirring once.

5. Remove the vegetables from the oven, place the steaks directly on top, and return to the oven. Roast until the desired doneness of your steak is reached, about 3 more minutes for medium-rare. Allow the steaks to rest before cutting.

NOTE: *To make this even faster, use quicker cooking vegetables like peppers, zucchini, or squash.*

Turkey with Mushrooms and Green Beans

What do you get when you combine leftover green bean casserole with turkey meat? We aren't sure, but this is kind of like what would happen if those two things got married and had a kid. Except without canned cream of something soup, and with no fried onions on the top (though see the note below about some crispy shallots). A question that used to get asked all the time in Paleo circles was "Aren't beans a no-no on Paleo?" With green beans, where you're eating more pod than bean, the potential deleterious effects are relatively negligible for most—and there's a whole lot of nutrient goodness in the shell. So eat away!

SERVES 3 TO 4 / PREP TIME: 5 MINUTES / TOTAL TIME: 20 MINUTES

2 tablespoons fat (olive oil, coconut oil, butter, or ghee)

2 shallots, sliced (see Notes)

8 ounces mushrooms, sliced (about 3 cups)

1 clove garlic, minced

1 pound turkey cutlets or breasts, cut into bite-size pieces

1 pound green beans, trimmed

1 teaspoon dried thyme

1 teaspoon dried rosemary

1 cup full-fat coconut milk or heavy cream

1. Heat a large skillet over medium-high heat. Add the fat and when hot but not smoking, add the shallots and sauté until just beginning to brown, 2 to 3 minutes. Add the mushrooms and garlic and cook until the mushrooms are just softened, 3 to 5 minutes.

2. Add the turkey and cook until the turkey is almost cooked through, 5 to 6 minutes longer.

3. Stir in the beans, thyme, rosemary, and coconut milk and cook uncovered until the beans are just softened, 3 to 4 minutes.

NOTES: *If you'd like to have some crispy shallots to serve on top, slice an extra shallot. In step 1, sauté all 3 shallots as directed and once they are softened, remove two-thirds of them and set aside. Then continue with the remaining shallot and cook until crispy. Set the crispy shallot aside, return the softened shallots to the pan, and continue with step 1.*

If you have leftover turkey or chicken, by all means use that in this dish!

Skillet Steaks with Veggies and Potatoes

This recipe makes use of the fond (the caramelized meat juices from the steak) to season the vegetables. The tanginess of the red wine vinegar mixed with some garlic and herbs makes for a great pairing with steak.

SERVES 6 TO 8 / PREP TIME: 10 MINUTES / TOTAL TIME: 30 MINUTES

2 pounds strip steaks, 1½ to 2 inches thick

Salt and black pepper

1 pound baby potatoes, halved or cut into ¼-inch slices (see Note)

3 tablespoons fat (olive oil, avocado oil, coconut oil, butter, or ghee)

1 yellow onion, diced

2 cloves garlic, minced

1 tablespoon red wine vinegar

1 red bell pepper, diced

2 medium zucchini, chopped

2 medium yellow squash, chopped

1 teaspoon dried rosemary

1 teaspoon dried thyme

1. Preheat the oven to 400°F.

2. Place the steaks on a plate and pat dry. Season with salt and black pepper.

3. Parcook the potatoes by placing them in a large, microwave-safe bowl and covering with water. Microwave on high for 7 minutes. Drain and slice into rounds about ¼ inch thick.

4. Heat a large ovenproof skillet over high heat. Add 1 tablespoon of the fat and when hot, add the steaks and sear for 3 to 4 minutes on each side. Remove to a plate and set aside.

5. Add the remaining 2 tablespoons fat to the pan and reduce the heat to medium-high. Add the potatoes, onion, and garlic and cook without stirring until slightly browned on the first side, 2 to 3 minutes. Stir in the vinegar, then add the bell pepper, zucchini, yellow squash, rosemary, and thyme, mixing well.

6. Set the steaks on top of the vegetables and place in the oven. Roast until the steaks reach desired doneness and the vegetables are softened, 8 to 10 minutes for medium rare. Season with salt and black pepper to taste.

NOTE: *If you do not tolerate white potatoes, simply omit them or use some cubed sweet potatoes instead.*

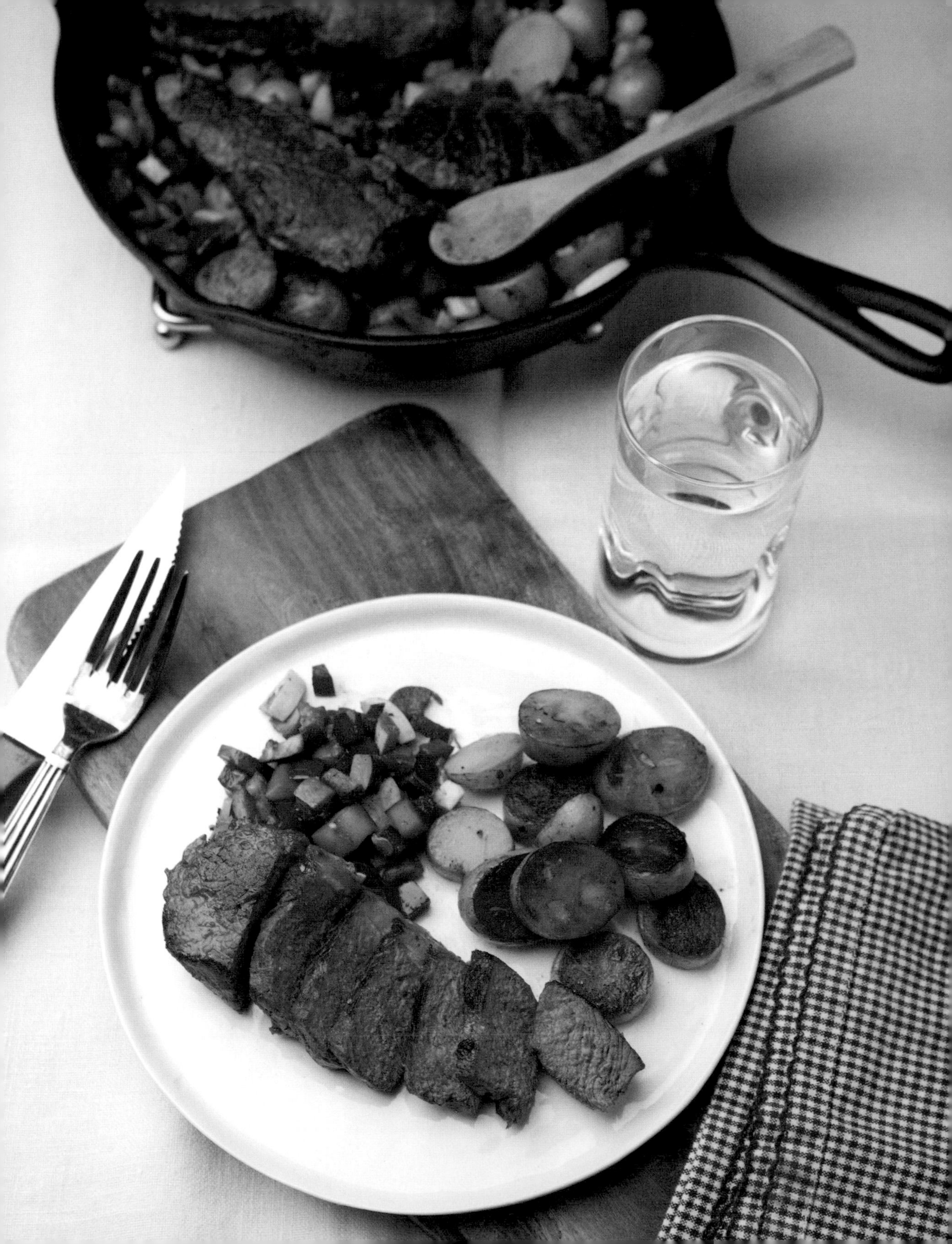

Turkey Cutlets with Stuffing

This is like a one-pot Thanksgiving meal without having to wait for a big turkey to be cooked. You can use any cuts of turkey meat or chicken for this, though cooking times will vary based on how thick your pieces are. We like to serve this with basic mashed cauliflower (page 99).

SERVES 3 TO 4 / PREP TIME: 10 MINUTES / TOTAL TIME: 30 MINUTES

1 tablespoon oil (olive, avocado, or coconut)

1 pound turkey cutlets

½ teaspoon salt

¼ teaspoon black pepper

3 ribs celery, diced

1 medium onion, chopped

2 cups sliced or chopped mushrooms

2 Granny Smith or other tart apples, cored and chopped

1 tablespoon chopped fresh sage or 1 teaspoon dried

1 tablespoon chopped fresh rosemary or 1 teaspoon dried

1 tablespoon chopped fresh thyme or 1 teaspoon dried

¼ cup chicken or turkey stock

1. Preheat the oven to 350°F.

2. Heat a large ovenproof skillet over medium-high heat and add the oil. While the oil heats, sprinkle the cutlets with the salt and pepper.

3. Add the cutlets to the hot oil and cook until just browned, 2 to 3 minutes per side. Remove to a plate.

4. Add the celery, onion, and mushrooms to the pan and stir, scraping up any of the browned bits from the turkey. Cook until the vegetables are softened, about 5 minutes.

5. Stir in the apples, sage, rosemary, thyme, and chicken stock. Place the turkey cutlets on top of the vegetable mixture, and place in the oven. Bake until turkey is cooked through, about 10 minutes.

VARIATION: *Some cooked, crumbled sausage mixed in with the vegetables adds even more depth to the stuffing-like creation. If you don't have turkey, chicken breasts (pounded into thin cutlets) or tenders would work just fine.*

Turkey or Chicken Pesto Pasta Bake

A few years ago Juli Bauer of PaleOMG posted the fantastic 5 Ingredient Pizza Spaghetti Pie recipe that was passed around the Internet like some Ryan Gosling meme. With all the fanfare, we just had to try it ourselves—it was delicious! The concept of that recipe (which is essentially spaghetti squash casserole) got us thinking about other ways in which we might make this—and lo and behold our pesto creation was born. And for a while at least, it was one of Scott's most favorite dishes.

SERVES 3 TO 4 / PREP TIME: 15 MINUTES / TOTAL TIME: 1 HOUR 30 MINUTES

2 small or 1 medium spaghetti squash (see Notes)

1½ cups lightly packed fresh basil

¼ cup pine nuts, walnuts, or other nuts of your choosing

Juice of ½ lemon

½ cup extra-virgin olive oil

Salt and black pepper

2 tablespoons fat (butter, ghee, coconut oil, avocado oil, or olive oil)

1½ pounds turkey or chicken breasts, sliced into bite-size pieces, or approximately 6 cups chopped, cooked chicken or turkey

4 large eggs

1. Preheat the oven to 400°F. Grease a large rectangular baking dish; 9 x 13-inch or 10 x 15-inch would both work fine.

2. Bake the spaghetti squash according to the oven method on page 102. Remove the squash from the oven and reduce the temperature to 375°F.

3. Meanwhile, in a food processor, combine the basil, nuts, and lemon juice and process until well combined. With the machine running, slowly add the olive oil to create a sauce-like consistency (because this will be added to the casserole you will want this to be runnier than a typical pesto). Season with salt and pepper to taste.

4. Heat a large skillet over medium-high heat. Add the fat and once hot, add the turkey and sauté until cooked through, 5 to 7 minutes.

5. Pull the spaghetti squash into strands and place in a large bowl. Add the pesto, turkey, and eggs. Pour the entire mixture into the baking dish.

6. Bake at 375°F until the casserole is set in the middle, about 1 hour.

NOTES: *If you have some already cooked spaghetti squash, this dish is incredibly quick to put together and bake. The leftovers taste just as good in our opinion. Spaghetti squash is really quick to cook in the Instant Pot. See page 102 for directions.*

VARIATIONS

This recipe can easily be tweaked for variety. Even in the basic recipe on page 135, we love to mix in some frozen spinach, halved cherry tomatoes, and/or some yellow squash or zucchini for extra veggies. Below are just a few examples of some ways to make this recipe almost entirely different:

Barbecue Bake: Use ½ cup barbecue sauce (your favorite or our recipe on page 216) instead of the pesto. Use the turkey or chicken as above, or use 1½ pounds (about 6 cups) cooked carnitas (page 73). Combine the spaghetti squash, barbecue sauce, carnitas, and eggs and bake as directed.

Vegetable Marinara Bake: Use ¾ cup marinara (your favorite or our 5-Ingredient Tomato sauce on page 214) instead of the pesto. Omit the turkey and in step 4, sauté 4 to 6 cups of your favorite vegetables (squash, zucchini, broccoli, peppers, onions) until slightly tender. Combine the spaghetti squash, marinara, vegetables, and eggs and bake as directed.

Tomato Meat Bake: Sauté 1 to 2 pounds of ground beef, turkey, or sausage in step 4, then add 3 to 4 cups of zucchini, summer squash, or your choice of vegetables and cook until softened. Combine the spaghetti squash, ¾ cup marinara, the meat and vegetable mixture, and eggs and bake as directed.

Spicy Sriracha Bake: Omit the pesto and combine ½ cup Sriracha-Sesame Mayonnaise (page 212) with 2 tablespoons Sriracha sauce. Omit the turkey and use 1½ pounds cooked shrimp or chicken. Combine the spaghetti squash, Sriracha mayo, 4 sliced green onions, and 3 eggs.

Shrimp and Okra Skillet

This is one of those "Oh man, we grew so much okra this year. What should we do with it?" recipes. We can only hope that for you okra fans out there you always have access to this vegetable! While oven-roasting okra is still one of our easiest and favorite ways to prepare it, we like coming up with new dishes that use this ingredient in ways you might not think of. This is just one such dish. The brightness of the lemon goes great with the shrimp, and the entire dish is on the table in less than 20 minutes.

SERVES 3 TO 4 / PREP TIME: 10 MINUTES / TOTAL TIME: 20 MINUTES

1 tablespoon oil (olive, avocado, or coconut)

1 pound okra, sliced lengthwise (see Note)

½ large onion, diced

2 cloves garlic, minced

1 cup sliced white mushrooms

½ teaspoon salt

1 pound shrimp, peeled and deveined

¼ cup chicken stock, store-bought or homemade (page 209)

Grated zest and juice of 1 lemon

1. Heat a large skillet over medium-high heat. Add the oil and when shimmering, add the okra and onion, stirring to coat with the oil. Cook until the okra has started to brown, about 5 minutes.

2. Stir in the garlic, mushrooms, and salt and cook another minute or two.

3. Stir in the shrimp, chicken stock, lemon zest, and lemon juice. Cook until the shrimp is just pink and cooked through, another 3 minutes or so.

NOTE: *When selecting okra, look for pods that are bright green without dark spots and are about 3 inches long. If the pod feels hard when you squeeze it, the okra will be woody and stringy, so avoid those. And don't be the person breaking off the tips of the okra pods (to test for woodiness) at your farmers' market or grocery store; you're not going to make many friends that way! We realize that not everyone likes okra like we do, because of the slime factor; the pan sautéing in this recipe minimizes the slime, so you may be won over! If you can't get your hands on okra, or you just don't like it, green beans, zucchini, or even carrots would work just fine.*

Basil-Ginger Pork

This is one of those recipes that's really good with regular (Italian) basil, but becomes exceptional if you can find and use Thai basil. Sadly, our local Asian market doesn't always carry the basil, and we don't always grow it . . . but when we can get our hands on it this is the first recipe I want to make. While this dish is a bit like the popular Thai larb dish, it's different enough that we didn't feel right calling it larb.

SERVES 3 TO 4 / PREP TIME: 10 MINUTES / TOTAL TIME: 25 MINUTES

1 pound ground pork

¼ cup coconut aminos

2 tablespoons Sriracha or a hot chili paste of your choosing

1 tablespoon sesame oil

1 tablespoon unseasoned rice vinegar

2 teaspoons fish sauce

2 tablespoons minced fresh ginger

2 cups cauliflower rice (see "How to Make Cauliflower Rice," page 30)

2 green onions, sliced on an angle

½ cup loosely packed fresh mint, coarsely chopped

½ cup loosely packed fresh Thai basil, coarsely chopped, or Italian basil

1 head Bibb lettuce or cabbage, for serving

1. Heat a large skillet over medium heat. Add the pork and cook until somewhat browned, 3 to 5 minutes.

2. Add in the aminos, Sriracha, sesame oil, rice vinegar, fish sauce, ginger, and cauliflower, and stir to combine well.

3. Reduce the heat to medium and continue cooking for 7 to 8 minutes to allow the flavors to combine and the cauliflower to soften, stirring as needed.

4. Mix in the green onions, mint, and basil and cook for 2 minutes longer. Serve atop lettuce leaves.

VARIATION: *Ground chicken or turkey also works well in this recipe.*

QUICKFIRE MEALS

The name says it all—these recipes are all pretty much under 30 minutes start to finish to help you get supper on the table in a flash.

Seafood Sunrises   143
Angry Clams   145
Avocado Soup with Scallops   146
Thai Fish Cakes   149
Chinois Chicken Salad   150
Trout in Parchment with Tomatoes and Basil Sauce   153
Crispy-Skinned Pan-Seared Salmon Fillets with
    Spicy Tomato Sauce   154
Macadamia-Crusted Halibut with Beurre Blanc and Cucumber
    Crabmeat Salad   155
An Assortment of Sauces for Fish   157
    Wasabi Mayonnaise   157
    Spicy Ginger Tomato Sauce   158
    Basil Sauce   158
    Anchovy-Garlic Sauce   159
    Olive Salsa   159
    Beurre Blanc   160
Chicken Salad Four Ways   161
    Traditional Chicken Salad   162
    Walnut Chicken Salad   163
    Buffalo Chicken Salad   165
    Warm Curry Chicken Salad   166
Chicken, Brussels Sprouts, and Bacon Skewers   169

Salmon with Blackberry Sauce   170

Summer Roll in a Bowl   173

Barbecue Shrimp Stew   174

Chicken with Peaches, Basil, and Tomatoes   177

Cube Steak with Mushrooms   179

Chop Chop Salad   180

Crab, Mango, and Jicama Salad   183

Veggie Steak Salad with Asian Dressing   184

Crispy Prosciutto Salad   186

Spicy Lamb Stir-Fry with Mint and Eggplant   188

Cucumber and Seafood Salad   189

Fish Burgers with Wasabi   190

Olive-Crusted Flounder   193

Sloppy Joes   194

Pan-Seared Frozen Steaks with Spinach-Artichoke Dip   197

Eggs Colorado   199

Pancetta-Wrapped Cod   201

Philly-Style Steak with Onions and Mushrooms   202

Spiced Pork Skillet   204

Seafood Sunrises

We usually try to get down to Mobile, Alabama, at least once a year. Not only is it incredibly relaxing to be by the water, but we always try to head on over to a little town called Bon Secour, where we load up on freshly caught shrimp and crab, not to mention the fun we have catching our own speck trout, flounder, and other fish in the bay. This recipe is inspired by the breakfasts we enjoy making down at the bay with all the fresh seafood.

SERVES 3 TO 4 / PREP TIME: 5 MINUTES / TOTAL TIME: 15 MINUTES

¼ pound bacon, diced

¼ cup chopped red onion

½ cup coarsely chopped white mushrooms

2 tablespoons butter

½ pound shrimp, peeled, deveined, and coarsely chopped

½ pound lump crabmeat

1 teaspoon Old Bay seasoning

4 large eggs

Salt and black pepper

1. In large skillet, fry the bacon over medium heat until cooked through, several minutes.

2. Add the onion, mushrooms, and 1 tablespoon of the butter. Sauté until the onions become translucent and slightly browned, about 5 minutes.

3. Add the remaining 1 tablespoon butter, the shrimp, crabmeat, and Old Bay. Cook until the shrimp are pink and fully cooked, 3 to 5 minutes (see Notes).

4. Make 4 indentations in the seafood and veggie mixture and crack an egg into each one. Reduce the heat to low, cover the skillet, and cook until the eggs are done to your liking, 3 to 4 minutes (less if you prefer runny yolks, longer if you prefer your yolks more cooked). Using a spatula, divide the pan into the 4 sections (each with 1 egg) and carefully spoon out each section. Season with salt and pepper.

NOTES: *You can make the seafood mixture a day or two in advance and have it ready to simply add to the skillet when breakfast time is short. We often double the seafood/veggie mixture and then use it as a stuffing for bell peppers or mushrooms.*

Feel free to substitute, add, or replace any of the seafood ingredients with your favorites. This is a great use for leftover cooked shrimp if you find yourself with any on hand!

Angry Clams

Don't let the name fool you: These clams are actually happy angry clams—the angry part just denotes their spicy nature. Clams are quite a happy protein choice as it relates to sustainability, and they are also a bit of a nutritional powerhouse. They're low in fat but high in protein, omega-3 fatty acids, and minerals like selenium, iron, and zinc. While we grew up loving clams in all sorts of preparations, we will admit that shucking clams is a labor of love. Here's a recipe where the heat of the pot does all the opening for you. Remember though: Any clams that don't open or that have a broken shell should be discarded.

SERVES 4 TO 6 / PREP TIME: 10 MINUTES / TOTAL TIME: 25 MINUTES

1 tablespoon coconut oil, olive oil, or other fat

1 onion, sliced

2 cloves garlic, minced

¼ pound bulk Mexican-style chorizo (though Spanish-style chorizo would also be fine; see Note)

1 tablespoon tomato paste

½ to 1 teaspoon crushed red pepper

½ cup dry white wine (or fish or chicken stock if avoiding wine)

1½ cups seafood or chicken stock

½ cup full-fat coconut milk

3 pounds fresh hard-shell clams (littleneck or cherrystones work well)

1. In a large Dutch oven or other pot with a lid, heat the oil over medium heat. Once shimmering, add the onion and sauté until softened and translucent, 3 to 4 minutes.

2. Add the garlic and chorizo and sauté until the chorizo is browned and fully cooked, 4 to 5 minutes. Use a wooden spoon to break the chorizo into small bits as it cooks.

3. Mix in the tomato paste and crushed red pepper and cook for a minute more. Pour in the wine, scraping up any of the browned bits on the bottom of the pan, then add the stock and coconut milk and stir.

4. Add the clams to the liquid mixture and stir to combine. Cover and cook until the clams open, 3 to 4 minutes. Serve hot.

NOTE: *Mexican chorizo (purchased as bulk sausage or as uncooked links) is quite different from Spanish-style chorizo, which is typically a hard cured or smoked ready-to-eat sausage. Both kinds are incredibly flavorful and tend to have a bit of a kick. If you decide to use the latter for this recipe, just make sure to remove any casing and reduce the amount of time needed to sauté as this kind is typically already fully cooked.*

Avocado Soup with Scallops

A creamy, cold soup that pairs exceptionally well with creamy scallops (or shrimp). Speedy tip: Place your ripe avocados in the refrigerator the day you know you'll be making this soup and you'll have already chilled soup as soon as you're done pureeing.

SERVES 4 AS A MAIN COURSE, 6 TO 8 AS AN APPETIZER / PREP TIME: 10 MINUTES / TOTAL TIME: 15 MINUTES, PLUS CHILLING TIME

FOR THE SOUP

3 medium Hass avocados, pitted and peeled

3 cups chicken stock, store-bought or homemade (page 209)

Juice of 2 limes

2 tablespoons chopped fresh cilantro, plus more for garnish

FOR THE SCALLOPS

1 pound dry-packed sea scallops, small side muscle removed

½ teaspoon ground cumin

¼ teaspoon cayenne pepper

¼ teaspoon chipotle powder

¼ teaspoon salt

1 tablespoon fat (butter, olive oil, or coconut oil)

1. To make the soup: In a blender, combine the avocados, chicken stock, lime juice, and cilantro and puree until smooth. Refrigerate until ready to serve.

2. Meanwhile, to make the scallops: Place the scallops on a paper towel and pat dry.

3. In a small bowl, combine the cumin, cayenne, chipotle powder, and salt. Sprinkle the spice mixture over both sides of the scallops.

4. Preheat a large skillet over medium-high heat. Add the fat and when hot, add the scallops to the pan. Let them cook undisturbed until you have a nice brown crust on the first side, 2 to 3 minutes. Flip the scallops and cook another 2 or so minutes, until almost cooked through (see Note). There will be some carryover cooking, so be careful not to overcook.

NOTE: *The size of your scallops will greatly impact cooking times. Large scallops are a special indulgence in our house.*

VARIATION: *Shrimp also pair beautifully with the soup, and the directions are almost exactly the same. The only difference is that you'll need to peel your shrimp first.*

Thai Fish Cakes

This is a dinner party favorite and can easily be made "fancier" by using some expensive crabmeat. Here we use canned tuna, which you're likely to have in your cupboard—or at least we recommend you have on hand for super-quick protein needs.

SERVES 4 TO 6 / PREP TIME: 20 MINUTES / TOTAL TIME: 35 MINUTES

Two 5-ounce cans wild-caught tuna (such as albacore) packed in water, drained

3 green onions, coarsely chopped

2 tablespoons finely chopped lemongrass

1 jalapeño pepper, seeded and finely chopped

1 tablespoon grated fresh ginger

1 tablespoon chopped fresh Italian (flat-leaf) parsley

1 large egg

½ cup cooked yuca root, mashed

Salt and black pepper

1 tablespoon coconut flour

¼ cup coconut oil

Dipping sauce of your choice, (such as the sauces on pages 211 to 220) or sambal oelek (or other chili paste)

1. In a large bowl, combine the tuna, green onions, lemongrass, jalapeño, ginger, parsley, and egg. Use your hands to combine well and then fold in the yuca.
2. Shape into patties and season each one with salt and black pepper, then dust with the coconut flour. Refrigerate for 15 minutes to allow them to set.
3. In a large skillet, heat the coconut oil over medium heat. Working in batches, fry the cakes until golden brown, 2 to 3 minutes per side. Remove the cooked cakes to a plate lined with paper towels to drain excess oil.
4. Serve with a dipping sauce or sambal oelek.

NOTE: *To save time, make the cakes through step 2 a day ahead and have them ready to serve in no time when guests arrive.*

VARIATION: *This recipe works with any flaky fish, crabmeat, or shrimp.*

Chinois Chicken Salad

When I lived in California, it was always a special treat to volunteer for the American Cancer Society's California Spirit gala, essentially a Taste of Los Angeles event. Chef Wolfgang Puck—arguably one of the pioneers of California fusion cuisine—was heavily involved, and his restaurant empire was well represented with delicious food to sample. Chef Puck's Chinois Chicken Salad is always one of the most popular dishes at the event, as it's been a staple menu item at many of his restaurants for decades. Here's our take inspired by his creation. While the recipe calls for "hot" mustard, if you cannot find it, use any powdered mustard.

—JULIE

SERVES 3 TO 4 / PREP TIME: 5 MINUTES / TOTAL TIME: 15 MINUTES

FOR THE DRESSING

2 teaspoons mustard powder (Chinese or English, such as Colman's, are best)

2 tablespoons sesame oil

2 tablespoons avocado oil

¼ cup unseasoned rice vinegar

1 teaspoon coconut aminos

1 teaspoon fish sauce

Salt and black pepper

FOR THE SALAD

1 head napa cabbage, chopped (see Note)

2 tablespoons butter or coconut oil

1 pound cooked chicken meat, shredded (about 4 cups)

½ cup snow peas, julienned

3 green onions, sliced on an angle

Toasted sesame seeds (optional)

1. To make the dressing: In a pint jar with a screw-top lid, combine the mustard powder, oils, vinegar, aminos, and fish sauce and shake well. Season with salt and pepper to taste.
2. To make the salad: Place the cabbage in a large bowl. Heat a large skillet over medium-high heat. Add the butter and when melted, add the chicken, stirring to coat well, and cook for 3 to 5 minutes, just enough to slightly brown the chicken (as it's already fully cooked).
3. Add the chicken, snow peas, green onions, sesame seeds (if using), and dressing to the cabbage and toss well.

NOTES: *The original Chinois Chicken Salad was a blend of romaine lettuce and cabbage—feel free to experiment with the greens that you most prefer.*
   Shrimp is also great in this instead of chicken, and julienned carrots or sweet bell peppers add some fun color, crunch, and flavor.

COOKING FISH

How to cook fish will depend on many factors: the thickness of the fish, the cut of a fish (steaks, fillets, whole), and honestly the kind of fish. Tuna, for example, is almost universally served rare, whereas swordfish steaks should be cooked through. So despite the fact that these two fish are both meatier fish, the preference for doneness makes a difference. Salmon is also typically served medium-rare, though some people always ask for theirs to be more well done. Delicate flounder or sole fillets are done in a matter of minutes. We could probably write an entire guide on cooking fish, but here's the abbreviated version:

For every inch of thickness of fish (measuring at the thickest part of the fish), cook for 10 minutes total (though we always suggest checking for doneness before that time is up—overcooked fish breaks our hearts). This applies to pretty much all methods of cooking (except low and slow smoking, and microwave cooking). So, for example, if you have a salmon fillet that is 1 inch thick, cook for 5 minutes on one side, flip over, and cook, starting to check after about 3 minutes (salmon is very often served at medium-rare, but if you prefer yours more well done, cook to your desired doneness). Generally speaking, very thin fish fillets need not be flipped over, and the fish is done when the flesh flakes easily with a fork.

Trout in Parchment with Tomatoes and Basil Sauce

While this recipe calls for trout fillets, you could just as easily use whole, butterflied trout.

SERVES 3 TO 4 / **PREP TIME: 5 MINUTES** / **TOTAL TIME: 15 MINUTES**

8 skin-on or skinless trout fillets (about 2 ounces each)

Basil Sauce (page 158)

2 large tomatoes, sliced

¼ cup fresh basil leaves

4 teaspoons olive oil

1. Preheat the oven to 375°F. Pull off 4 large pieces of parchment paper (or foil).

2. Fold a piece of parchment in half, making a crease, then open the parchment like a book. Place 2 fillets on the same side of the crease. Repeat with the remaining parchment and fish fillets.

3. Spoon about 1 tablespoon basil sauce over the fillets in each packet. Top the fillets with a few tomato slices and a few basil leaves, then drizzle the tomatoes in each packet with 1 teaspoon olive oil.

4. Fold the parchment over the top of the fish/tomato mixture and seal the packages by crimping the edges together.

5. Place the packets on a baking sheet and bake until the fish flakes easily, about 10 minutes.

6. Serve with more basil sauce.

VARIATION: *Make it a meal! Place some vegetables, like sliced zucchini or summer squash, spinach, or kale under the trout in the packets in step 1 and you have a full meal in a packet.*

Crispy-Skinned Pan-Seared Salmon Fillets with Spicy Tomato Sauce

While we use the Spicy Ginger Tomato Sauce (page 158) here, any of the sauces from pages 157 to 160 would be great.

SERVES 3 TO 4 / PREP TIME: 5 MINUTES / TOTAL TIME: 15 MINUTES

1 pound skin-on salmon fillets, cut into 3 or 4 pieces

Salt and black pepper

2 tablespoons oil (coconut, olive, or avocado)

Spicy Ginger Tomato Sauce (page 158)

1. Dry the salmon fillets on all sides with paper towels. Liberally sprinkle the fleshy side with the salt and pepper.
2. Heat a stainless steel skillet over medium-high heat. Add the oil and when shimmering, add the fish fillets skin side down. Immediately reduce the heat to medium-low and cook, pressing down on the fillets with a spatula to ensure even crisping of the skin, until the skin is crispy and the salmon easily releases from the pan, 6 to 7 minutes (if it is sticking at all, then let it cook a minute or two longer).
3. Flip over and cook for a minute or two longer, until an instant-read thermometer registers 130°F for medium-rare doneness.
4. Serve topped with the tomato sauce.

Macadamia-Crusted Halibut with Beurre Blanc and Cucumber Crabmeat Salad

If you don't have halibut or you find its price tag prohibitive, try this with cod, haddock, turbot, or striped bass.

SERVES 4 / PREP TIME: 5 MINUTES / TOTAL TIME: 25 MINUTES

4 skinless halibut fillets (about 4 to 6 ounces each)

¾ cup unsalted macadamia nuts, finely chopped

¼ cup unsweetened shredded coconut

1 tablespoon fat (melted coconut oil, ghee, or butter)

Salt and black pepper

Beurre Blanc (page 160)

Cucumber and Seafood Salad, made with crabmeat (page 189)

1. Preheat the oven to 400°F. Line a baking sheet with foil.
2. Place the halibut fillets on the baking sheet and roast for 8 minutes.
3. Meanwhile, in a small bowl, combine the nuts, coconut, and melted fat, and salt and pepper to taste.
4. Remove the fish from the oven and evenly distribute the nut mixture over the 4 fillets, pressing to help it adhere. Return to the oven and roast until fish flakes easily and is cooked through, another 5 to 10 minutes.
5. Serve the fish on top of the beurre blanc or pour the sauce over the fish. Serve the salad on the side.

ANCHOVY-GARLIC SAUCE

OLIVE SALSA

SPICY GINGER
TOMATO SAUCE

WASABI
MAYONNAISE

BEURRE BLANC

An Assortment of Sauces for Fish

Being landlocked here in Tennesee, we do our best to seize the opportunity to stockpile our freezer with the fresh catch of the day when down in Mobile, Alabama, or when fish is on sale at our local grocers. Sustainability is important to us, so we typically check the Monterey Bay Aquarium's Seafood Watch list to ensure we are being as environmentally responsible as possible (and we might suggest you do the same). See the resources section for our recommendations on seafood sources.

In addition to having numerous nutritional benefits, fish is also one of the quickest proteins to cook up for dinnertime (and we mean besides the frozen fish sticks many of us grew up with). Topped with one of the sauces that follow, you're sure to please a crowd. The directions are simple: Choose what fish you'd like to cook (or, if you're like us, what you have on hand and in the freezer), what method you'd like to use (sautéed, poached, grilled, oven-roasted [see page 152 for guidelines]), then choose which sauce sounds best to you. These sauces can work on heartier, meatier fish like swordfish, tuna, or salmon, but they also are delicious on trout, flounder, or bass, or even shellfish like shrimp or scallops. Check out the other mayonnaise recipes on pages 211 to 213 for even more sauce ideas.

Wasabi Mayonnaise

Careful on the wasabi—too much can clear out your sinuses for days! This sauce goes exceptionally well with tuna steaks (tuna and wasabi are a match made in heaven!); it's also delicious on nonfishy proteins like burgers or grilled chicken.

MAKES ½ CUP / PREP TIME: 5 MINUTES / TOTAL TIME: 5 MINUTES

½ cup mayonnaise, store-bought or homemade (page 211)

1 teaspoon wasabi powder (or more to your liking)

1 teaspoon minced fresh ginger

1 teaspoon fresh lemon juice

In a small bowl, combine all the ingredients. You can make the sauce in advance and store it for up to 1 week in the refrigerator.

Spicy Ginger Tomato Sauce

Serve this hot sauce poured over fish like pan-seared swordfish steaks, oven-roasted flounder, or sautéed sole. It goes great over chicken and shrimp too!

MAKES 1 CUP / PREP TIME: 5 MINUTES / TOTAL TIME: 10 MINUTES

1 tablespoon olive oil

1 clove garlic, minced

2 teaspoons minced fresh ginger

¼ to ½ teaspoon crushed red pepper (or more for a more spicy sauce)

1 cup peeled tomatoes (canned or fresh)

1. In a saucepan, combine all the ingredients and bring to a simmer over medium heat.
2. Transfer to a blender or food processor and blend until smooth. You can make the sauce in advance and store it for up to 1 week in the refrigerator.

Basil Sauce

The mayo makes for a really creamy sauce that goes perfectly on top of salmon, tuna, or even steak. You can also use it as a dipping sauce for cherry tomatoes or other vegetables.

MAKES ABOUT ¾ CUP / PREP TIME: 5 MINUTES / TOTAL TIME: 5 MINUTES

⅔ cup mayonnaise, store-bought or homemade (page 211)

¼ cup fresh basil leaves

1 clove garlic, mashed into a paste

2 tablespoons olive oil

½ teaspoon fresh lemon juice

In a small food processor or blender, combine all the ingredients. You can make the sauce in advance and store it for up to 1 week in the refrigerator.

Anchovy-Garlic Sauce

Don't let the anchovies scare you! Serve the sauce, still warm, over any fish, but over salmon it makes for a super-rich and decadent meal.

MAKES ½ CUP / PREP TIME: 5 MINUTES / TOTAL TIME: 10 MINUTES

2 cloves garlic, mashed into a paste

1 tablespoon chopped rinsed anchovy fillets (3 or 4)

4 tablespoons butter or ghee

¼ cup extra-virgin olive oil

1 teaspoon lemon zest

3 to 4 teaspoons fresh lemon juice

Salt and pepper

In a small saucepan, combine the garlic, anchovies, butter, olive oil, lemon zest, and 3 teaspoons of the lemon juice. Taste and add more lemon juice if needed, and season with salt and pepper to taste. You can make the sauce in advance and store it for up to 1 week in the refrigerator.

Olive Salsa

MAKES ABOUT ½ CUP / PREP TIME: 5 MINUTES / TOTAL TIME: 5 MINUTES

½ cup cherry or grape tomatoes, quartered, or 1 large tomato, seeded and diced (about ½ cup)

1 clove garlic, minced

2 tablespoons pitted and chopped kalamata olives

1 tablespoon minced fresh Italian (flat-leaf) parsley

1 teaspoon grated orange zest

2 teaspoons capers, rinsed

2 tablespoons olive oil

In a bowl, combine all the ingredients and keep refrigerated until ready to serve. You can make the sauce in advance and store it for up to 1 week in the refrigerator.

Beurre Blanc

This is the only one of the sauces that is near to impossible to make ahead of time and not have break on you. If it's too warm, it breaks, and if it's too cold, it also breaks. While traditional beurre blanc does not incorporate heavy cream or coconut milk, we find that it helps to stabilize the sauce some and can help with a broken sauce. In the event your sauce breaks, see the note on how to fix it. Beurre blanc goes great with just about any fish you can think of—salmon, trout, snapper, sole, tuna—and is a decadent accompaniment for lobster!

MAKES ABOUT ½ CUP / PREP TIME: 5 MINUTES / TOTAL TIME: 15 MINUTES

¼ cup white wine (or if you avoid wine: 2 tablespoons white wine vinegar and 2 tablespoons chicken stock; but it tastes way better with wine)

2 sprigs fresh thyme

1 shallot, coarsely chopped

2 tablespoons heavy cream or full-fat coconut milk

4 tablespoons cold unsalted butter, cubed

Salt and white pepper

1. In a small saucepan, combine the wine, thyme, and shallot over medium-high heat and bring to a boil. Allow to boil until reduced to about 1 tablespoon, about 5 minutes. Strain out the thyme and shallot.

2. Add the cream and whisk for a minute more.

3. Reduce the heat to low and, whisking constantly, slowly add the butter, one cube at a time, until fully incorporated.

4. Season with salt and white pepper to taste. Serve immediately, while still warm.

WHAT TO DO IF YOUR BEURRE BLANC BREAKS

Should you find yourself with a beurre blanc that looks more like melted butter mixed with some stuff, that means your sauce has broken. The sauce can break when you add too much butter at once, when the butter's not cold enough, or when you don't whisk it fast enough. While it still tastes delicious, to get the right mouthfeel and appearance, you'll want to blend it back together. To do so, take the pan off the heat and try vigorously whisking in just a few ice chips; some people also have success using an immersion blender.

Chicken Salad Four Ways

It's hard not to love the ease of chicken salad. We almost always have some already cooked chicken in our refrigerator, as it's such a great ingredient to have on hand for the kids, to use in frittatas or in Cauliflower Egg Muffins (page 107), or in any of the chicken salad recipes you'll find here. Our leftover meat usually comes from our own whole-roasted or slow-cooked chickens, but any chicken meat will do. Sometimes that might mean a rotisserie chicken from the grocery store, and while those rotisserie birds aren't typically pasture-raised, if it's eating a lesser quality bird vs. going completely off the Paleo reservation, we'll stick to the former. When you buy a store-bought bird, be sure to check the label for any ingredients you may want to avoid.

In the following pages we dish up a few twists on the old favorite.

WALNUT CHICKEN SALAD

BUFFALO CHICKEN SALAD

TRADITIONAL CHICKEN SALAD

Traditional Chicken Salad

You can get into some heated arguments over the proper way to make chicken salad. That's one of the several reasons we have a few variations in the book. Even among our family, there is debate over chunky or smooth. Heck, our dear friend Chris Hall refuses to add grapes to chicken salad. As there are so many ways to make chicken salad, it's a prime reason we suggest always roasting more than one chicken, to ensure you always have ample cooked chicken on hand.

SERVES 3 TO 4 / PREP TIME: 10 MINUTES / TOTAL TIME: 10 MINUTES

4 cups shredded or diced cooked chicken

1 cup chopped celery

½ cup chopped white onion

¼ cup minced fresh Italian (flat-leaf) parsley

½ cup mayonnaise, store-bought or homemade (page 211)

1 tablespoon yellow mustard

Salt and black pepper

Lettuce and sliced tomatoes or cucumbers, for serving

1. In a food processor (see Notes), combine the chicken, celery, onion, parsley, mayo, and mustard and pulse to desired consistency.

2. Season with salt and pepper to taste and serve on a bed of lettuce along with tomatoes or cucumbers.

NOTES: *Some like it chunky, some like it smooth. If you're a chunky chicken salad eater, no real need to even use the food processor. Just mix thoroughly in a bowl. This recipe can be easily scaled up or down based on the amount of leftover chicken you have.*

Walnut Chicken Salad

While some people like a "smoother" chicken salad, this one begs to be chunky, playing off the crunch of the celery and walnuts. —**CHARLES**

SERVES 3 TO 4 / PREP TIME: 10 MINUTES / TOTAL TIME: 10 MINUTES

3 cups diced cooked chicken meat

1 rib celery, minced

½ cup walnuts, chopped

½ cup raisins

⅓ cup mayonnaise, store-bought or homemade (page 211)

1 tablespoon Dijon mustard

1 tablespoon apple cider vinegar

1 tablespoon finely chopped fresh tarragon

¼ teaspoon sea salt

¼ teaspoon cracked black pepper

Pinch of garlic powder

Lettuce or sliced tomatoes, zucchini, or cucumber, for serving

1. In a large bowl, combine the chicken, celery, walnuts, raisins, mayo, mustard, vinegar, tarragon, salt, pepper, and garlic powder and mix thoroughly.

2. Serve on lettuce or with sliced tomatoes, zucchini, or cucumber.

Buffalo Chicken Salad

A cool chicken salad with a nice kick. Use your favorite hot sauce to give this the kick you want. Use either leftover poached chicken (page 31) or leftover roasted chicken (page 26) to get this one put together in just a few minutes.

SERVES 3 TO 4 / PREP TIME: 10 MINUTES / TOTAL TIME: 10 MINUTES

4 cups shredded or diced cooked chicken

1 sweet potato, cooked, peeled, and cut into small chunks (optional)

3 ribs celery, chopped

3 green onions, thinly sliced (about ⅔ cup)

½ cup mayonnaise, store-bought or homemade (page 211)

¼ cup Buffalo wing hot sauce or other hot sauce of your choosing (more or less depending upon preference)

Salt and black pepper

Place the chicken, sweet potato (if using), celery, green onions, mayo, and Buffalo sauce in a large bowl and mix well. Season with salt and pepper to taste.

VARIATION: *Use Sriracha (about 2 tablespoons) instead of the hot sauce and add 1 teaspoon of sesame oil for a fun twist.*

Warm Curry Chicken Salad

While you could certainly use leftover chicken to make this recipe, we find that freshly cooked and still-warm chicken really helps the flavors meld.

SERVES 6 TO 8 / PREP TIME: 10 MINUTES / TOTAL TIME: 25 MINUTES

2 tablespoons coconut oil

2 pounds boneless, skinless chicken breast, cut into 1-inch cubes

1 teaspoon salt

2 tablespoons Thai yellow curry paste

1 cup full-fat coconut milk

1 cup chopped sweet onion

1 cup dried currants (see Notes)

1 cup chicken stock, store-bought or homemade (page 209)

1 tart apple, peeled, cored, and coarsely chopped

½ cup chopped fresh cilantro

½ cup chopped green onions

¼ cup mayonnaise, store-bought or homemade (page 211)

1. In a large skillet, heat the coconut oil over medium heat. When hot, add the chicken and cook until the meat is no longer pink and the juices run clear, about 8 minutes. Add the salt and mix well. Remove the chicken with a slotted spoon and set aside in a large bowl.

2. Keeping the heat on medium, add the curry paste to the pan. As it's getting fragrant, pour in the coconut milk and combine well. Add the onion and cook until softened, about 5 minutes.

3. Add the currants and stock, reducing the heat to a simmer. When the currants begin to plump up, remove the pan from the heat and pour the mixture over the chicken, tossing to combine well.

4. Stir in the apple, cilantro, green onions, and mayonnaise and toss well. Serve immediately.

NOTES: *If you don't have currants, raisins work just fine. You can also use a large Dutch oven instead of a skillet. And if you don't have a large enough cooking vessel, cook the chicken in batches.*

✱ NOTES: *Metal skewers are easier than wooden ones for poking through the tough Brussels sprouts. Also, most bacon will add a good amount of salt to this dish, so you may wish to omit the additional salt.*

Chicken, Brussels Sprouts, and Bacon Skewers

Is there a better pairing than Brussels sprouts and bacon? Here we harness the smoky bacon flavor and combine that with some sweet balsamic vinegar and tangy mustard to make this a complete meal on a stick. While we wish we could take credit for the idea of Brussels sprouts on a skewer with bacon wrapped around them, this one hails from Charles's mom and her lunch bunch crew. These skewers can easily be done without the chicken, and are especially tasty with some shallots or pieces of onions threaded onto the skewers.

SERVES 3 TO 4 AS A MAIN COURSE / PREP TIME: 10 MINUTES / TOTAL TIME: 25 TO 30 MINUTES

1 tablespoon Dijon mustard

¼ cup balsamic vinegar

¼ cup olive oil

1 pound boneless, skinless chicken breasts or thighs, cut into 30 to 35 bite-size pieces

½ pound bacon (NOT very thick cut), halved lengthwise

2 pounds Brussels sprouts, trimmed

¼ teaspoon salt (optional; see Notes opposite)

¼ teaspoon black pepper

1. Preheat the oven to 400°F.

2. In a medium bowl, whisk together the mustard, vinegar, and oil. Measure out 2 tablespoons of the mixture and set aside.

3. Add the chicken to the bowl, tossing with the dressing. Allow to sit for at least a few minutes.

4. To build the skewers (see Notes opposite): Thread one end of a bacon strip onto a skewer. Alternate threading Brussels sprouts and chicken pieces until the skewer has about 4 or 5 Brussels sprouts and the same number of pieces of chicken. Twirling in a candy cane fashion, wrap the bacon around the exterior of the Brussels sprouts and chicken, threading the other end of the bacon strips onto the end of the skewer to finish off. Repeat using the remaining ingredients. You should end up with 8 to 10 skewers.

5. Brush the skewers with the reserved mustard/balsamic/olive oil mixture and sprinkle all with the salt (if using) and pepper.

6. Arrange the skewers on a rimmed baking sheet and bake until the bacon is slightly crispy and the chicken cooked through, 15 to 20 minutes.

Salmon with Blackberry Sauce

We're always super excited when summertime rolls around, which means it's time to go pick berries up at the family farm. Our son, Scott, loves to pick "backuhberries" at his uncle Michael's, and this sauce is a perfect way for us to use up some of the bounty.

SERVES 3 TO 4 / PREP TIME: 15 MINUTES / TOTAL TIME: 25 MINUTES

2 cups blackberries, fresh or frozen

1-inch piece fresh ginger, minced

Juice of ½ lemon

1 tablespoon honey (optional)

1 tablespoon oil (coconut, avocado, or olive)

4 salmon fillets (4 to 6 ounces each), skin-on or skinless

1. In a small saucepan, combine the blackberries, ginger, lemon juice, honey (if using), and 1 cup water. Bring to a simmer over medium heat, using a fork or potato masher to mash the blackberries as the sauce cooks. Simmer until the berries have mostly broken down, about 5 minutes.

2. Pour the sauce contents into a blender or small food processor and process until smooth. Strain through a fine-mesh sieve, pushing down on the solids to extract as much sauce as possible. Set aside.

3. Heat a large cast-iron or stainless steel skillet over medium-high heat. Add the oil and when shimmering, add the salmon (skin side down if using skin-on). Reduce the heat to medium-low and cook undisturbed for 6 to 7 minutes on the first side. Use a spatula to flip the salmon and cook a minute or two longer on the other side until an instant-read thermometer registers your desired internal temperature (130°F for medium).

4. Serve topped with some of the blackberry sauce.

VARIATIONS: *Raspberries and blueberries are also great in this sauce, and we love it over chicken too.*

Summer Roll in a Bowl

Vietnamese summer rolls (*gỏi cuốn*) were the standard by which I measured all Vietnamese restaurants back in my LA days. Restaurants that skimped on the shrimp were not on my favorites list, and quite a few were blacklisted due to their egregious tofu ways. Of course, those with great dipping sauces got high marks, because sauces always win me over. And then I danced happy dances when I realized many Thai restaurants served a version of these, too. Having attempted to make summer rolls on my own with those tricky rice paper wrappers, I decided they just weren't worth the hassle (soaking in the warm water, sometimes too long, sometimes not enough, getting stuck to everything etc.), so I skip the wrapper, toss everything in a bowl, and call it good. **—JULIE**

SERVES 3 TO 4 / PREP TIME: 10 MINUTES / TOTAL TIME: 15 MINUTES

1 pound medium shrimp, peeled and deveined

1 mango, peeled and pitted, cut into chunks

1 teaspoon sambal oelek, chili garlic sauce, or Sriracha sauce

1 tablespoon fresh lime juice

Various lettuce leaves (Bibb, romaine, etc.)

Leaves from 4 to 5 sprigs fresh Thai basil (about 40)

Leaves from 4 to 5 sprigs fresh mint (about 30)

1 English cucumber, seeded and cut into 2-inch long pieces

½ cup bean sprouts

1 green onion, sliced

1. Bring a medium pot of water to a boil over high heat. Add the shrimp and cook until just pink and cooked through, about 3 minutes. Drain in a colander and rinse under cold water.

2. Meanwhile, in a small food processor or blender, combine the mango, sambal oelek, and lime juice and process until smooth. Taste and adjust seasonings as desired.

3. To serve, line a bowl with the lettuce leaves (see Note). Top with the shrimp, Thai basil, mint, cucumber, sprouts, and green onion. Serve the mango sauce alongside.

VARIATIONS: *Cooked pork and rice noodles are two very typical ingredients in this dish, so feel free to include.*

NOTE: *Of course you can plate this for individuals as you like. Just divide the lettuce leaves among 3 or 4 individual bowls in step 3, then evenly divide the shrimp, Thai basil, mint, cucumber, sprouts, and green onions among all. Serve the dipping sauce for sharing or in individual ramekins.*

Barbecue Shrimp Stew

This is like barbecue meets gumbo—almost a cross between Brunswick stew and some New Orleans flavors. It's not a spicy stew—unless you want it to be—in which case we suggest using more cayenne pepper.

SERVES 6 TO 8 / PREP TIME: 10 MINUTES / TOTAL TIME: 30 MINUTES

1 tablespoon lard or bacon drippings

¼ cup arrowroot starch/flour

1 green bell pepper, finely chopped

1 medium onion, coarsely chopped

1 rib celery, finely chopped

2 cloves garlic, minced

2 cups okra, cut into ½-inch lengths

1 cup diced tomatoes

2 cups vegetable stock

1 cup barbecue sauce, store-bought or homemade (page 216)

¼ teaspoon cayenne pepper

½ teaspoon salt

2 pounds shrimp, peeled and deveined

1. In a Dutch oven, heat the lard over medium heat until hot.

2. Add the arrowroot starch/flour and stir frequently with a wooden spoon until golden brown, 3 to 5 minutes, being careful not to burn the roux.

3. Stir in the bell pepper, onion, celery, and garlic and sauté until the onion begins to soften, about 5 minutes.

4. Add the okra, tomatoes, stock, and barbecue sauce. Bring the mixture to a boil and stir in the cayenne and salt.

5. Reduce the heat to medium-low, add the shrimp, and cook, stirring frequently, until the shrimp are pink and opaque, about 6 minutes.

VARIATIONS: *Scallops, crabmeat, and clams all make great substitutions here.*

Chicken with Peaches, Basil, and Tomatoes

Summertime in the South brings with it two of our favorite things: peaches and tomatoes. While I still don't love biting into a whole tomato as much as I do a whole peach, I do love both of these fruits in so many preparations, and together they add a lovely sweet flavor to the chicken. Served over peppery arugula, this makes for a great weeknight meal in a flash. This recipe was inspired by a similar dish from Virginia Willis's James Beard Award–winning book, *Lighten Up, Y'all.*   **—JULIE**

SERVES 6 TO 8 / PREP TIME: 10 MINUTES / TOTAL TIME: 25 MINUTES

1 tablespoon fat (coconut oil, olive oil, or ghee)

1½ to 2 pounds boneless, skinless chicken breasts or thighs

1 teaspoon salt

½ teaspoon black pepper

1 shallot, sliced

2 cloves garlic, thinly sliced

2 teaspoons minced fresh ginger

3 peaches, pitted and sliced

2 medium tomatoes, cut into wedges

1 cup chicken stock, store-bought or homemade (page 209)

2 tablespoons finely chopped fresh basil

6 to 8 ounces arugula

1. Heat a large cast-iron or stainless steel skillet over medium-high heat and add the fat (see Note). While the fat is heating, season the chicken with the salt and pepper. When the fat is hot and shimmering (not smoking), add the chicken and sear, undisturbed, on the first side until golden brown, 2 to 3 minutes. Flip and cook for another 2 minutes. Remove the chicken to a plate.

2. Reduce the heat to medium and add the shallot to the pan. Sauté until slightly softened, then mix in the garlic and ginger and sauté a minute more.

3. Stir in the peaches, tomatoes, chicken stock, and 1 tablespoon of the basil. Return the chicken to the pan, spooning some of the juices over the chicken.

4. Cover and simmer the chicken until cooked through, 10 to 15 minutes.

5. Serve over the arugula, with the sauce poured over like a dressing, and garnish with the remaining basil.

NOTE: *You can cook this entire dish from start to finish in the oven (400°F for 15 to 20 minutes), but we prefer the flavor of the sautéed shallots and browned exterior of the chicken. You can also cook on the stovetop through step 3, then put the entire pan in a 350°F oven in step 4 and bake until the chicken is cooked through, 10 to 15 minutes.*

Cube Steak with Mushrooms

For as long as I can remember, I would always request my venison tenderloins whole when I harvested a deer. My brother, on the other hand, loves cube steak and would request to have all of his processed in that fashion. I think he might have been on to something, as I've learned that you can sneak a whole lot of flavor and texture into the crevices of this cut of meat. If you don't have access to venison, or aren't a fan, this recipe works equally well with beef.

—CHARLES

SERVES 4 / PREP TIME: 5 MINUTES / TOTAL TIME: 20 MINUTES

4 beef or venison cube steaks, about 4 to 5 ounces each (see Note)

½ teaspoon salt

¼ teaspoon cracked black pepper

Dash of ground cinnamon

1 tablespoon coconut flour

1 tablespoon coconut oil

2 teaspoons Dijon mustard

1 tablespoon ghee

1 pound mushrooms, sliced

¼ medium onion, chopped

1 clove garlic, minced

¼ cup beef or chicken stock

1 tablespoon coconut aminos

2 tablespoons minced fresh Italian parsley

1. Season both sides of the cube steak with the salt, pepper, and cinnamon. Dust both sides with the coconut flour.
2. In large skillet, heat the coconut oil over medium heat. Add the steaks and cook until browned, about 3 minutes per side. Remove the steaks to a plate and spread ½ teaspoon mustard on each one.
3. Add the ghee to the skillet over medium heat. Add the mushrooms, onion, and garlic and sauté for about 5 minutes or until the mushrooms begin to soften. Add the stock and stir to deglaze the pan.
4. Stir in the coconut aminos and parsley, then return the steaks to the skillet. Cover and simmer until cooked through, about 6 to 8 minutes.
5. Serve the steaks topped with the mushrooms, with your favorite veggies on the side.

NOTE: *This recipe works really well for pan-frying traditional steaks too. You can tenderize them with a studded kitchen mallet or keep the steaks in their original form.*

Chop Chop Salad

Charles's mom heard of this salad via one of her "lunch bunch" ladies—a dynamic group of women who have been friends for decades. Choose greens that have some crunch to them or are relatively hearty and won't wilt overnight (as you may have leftovers). The best part? The Caesar-ish Dressing, which is egg-and-dairy-free, but still creamy and flavorful enough to make you think you're eating a salad with a Caesar dressing.

SERVES 6 TO 8 / PREP TIME: 10 MINUTES / TOTAL TIME: 15 MINUTES

2 romaine lettuce hearts, washed and chopped into bite-size pieces (about 8 cups)

1 cup cherry tomatoes, quartered

¼ pound bacon, cooked until crispy and chopped into small pieces

1½ pounds cooked chicken, chopped

2 avocados, pitted and diced

½ cup store-bought Paleo-friendly Caesar dressing (Tessemae's is totally Paleo *and* egg-free) or our Caesar-ish Dressing (recipe follows)

Place all the chopped ingredients in a large bowl and toss with the dressing. It's that easy!

NOTE: *If you want to make the salad ahead of time, assemble everything except the avocado and dressing. Then stir in the avocado at the last minute and toss everything with the dressing.*

VARIATIONS: *Try prosciutto instead of bacon. Or add some feta cheese (and reduce the amount of dressing).*

Caesar-ish Dressing

MAKES 1 CUP DRESSING / PREP TIME: 5 MINUTES / TOTAL TIME: 5 MINUTES

1 avocado, pitted and peeled

4 anchovy fillets, rinsed

Juice of ½ lemon

1 clove garlic, peeled and smashed

2 tablespoons extra-virgin olive oil or avocado oil

1 teaspoon Dijon mustard (optional)

In a food processor or blender combine all the ingredients and puree. Add more oil if you want a thinner consistency.

Crab, Mango, and Jicama Salad

Crab is one of those "luxury" purchases for us (jumbo lump blue crabmeat is often around $20/pound), so when we eat it, we want to make sure that its delicate flavor is the star of the show. This is probably why the West Indies Salad (which originated in Mobile, Alabama, in the 1940s, not in the West Indies) is so darn popular in the South: The salad is basically a mix of crab, onion, vinegar, and oil, and the crabmeat is center stage. While we're fans of simplicity, we also like to jazz up our crab-based meals, so here we mix in some juicy mango and jicama for the crunch, and use some red onion to add a little more flavor. You can just as easily use some fresh peaches (for the sweet) and some cucumber in place of the jicama (for the crunch).

**SERVES 3 TO 4 AS A MAIN COURSE, 6 TO 8 AS AN APPETIZER / PREP TIME: 10 MINUTES /
TOTAL TIME: 10 MINUTES**

1 pound crabmeat, picked over for shells

2 mangoes, peeled and cut into ¼-inch dice

1 jicama, peeled and cut into ¼-inch dice

¼ cup chopped fresh cilantro

¼ red or sweet yellow onion, finely minced (optional)

2 tablespoons fresh lime juice

3 tablespoons apple cider vinegar

3 tablespoons avocado oil or olive oil

1. In a large bowl, combine the crabmeat, mangoes, jicama, cilantro, and onion and gently combine (if you paid the pretty penny for lump crabmeat you want to keep those lumps, well, lumpy!).

2. In a separate bowl, combine the lime juice, vinegar, and oil, and whisk to combine well.

3. Pour the mixture over the crab salad and stir to incorporate.

4. Keep refrigerated until ready to serve.

VARIATION: *Shrimp and lobster are great options, or if you can find only canned crab, that works too.*

Veggie Steak Salad with Asian Dressing

Some folks in the Paleosphere like to use the hashtag #morevegetablesthanavegetarian and this one certainly fits the bill. Don't let the ingredient list deter you—most Paleo pantries are well stocked with these.

SERVES 4 TO 6 / PREP TIME: 10 MINUTES / TOTAL TIME: 20 MINUTES, PLUS RESTING TIME

FOR THE STEAK

One 1½-pound sirloin or flank steak, about 1 inch thick, brought to room temperature

1 teaspoon Chinese five-spice powder

¾ teaspoon salt

½ teaspoon black pepper

FOR THE DRESSING

¼ cup almond butter or other nut or seed butter of your choosing

¼ cup avocado oil or olive oil

2 tablespoons fresh lime juice

2 tablespoons unseasoned rice vinegar

1 tablespoon coconut aminos

1 tablespoon honey

2 teaspoons fish sauce

1-inch piece fresh ginger, coarsely chopped

1 clove garlic, chopped

1 tablespoon chopped fresh cilantro

Salt and black pepper

FOR THE SALAD

1 head napa cabbage or savoy cabbage, sliced crosswise

1 red bell pepper, cut into strips

1 green bell pepper, cut into strips

1 medium daikon, peeled and cut into matchsticks

1 English cucumber, peeled and cut into matchsticks

1 mango, peeled, pitted, and cut into matchsticks

4 green onions, sliced on an angle

1. Preheat the broiler to high and position the rack about 6 inches away from the heating element. Or preheat an outdoor grill to medium high heat (direct heat for charcoal).

2. Season the steak with the Chinese five-spice powder, salt, and pepper.

3. Place the steak on a broiler pan or in a broilerproof skillet and broil for about 4 minutes per side for medium-rare (see Note). If grilling, grill over direct heat and cook for 3 or 4 minutes per side. Allow the steak to rest about 10 minutes.

4. While the steak is resting, make the dressing: In a small food processor or blender, combine the almond butter, oil, lime juice, vinegar, aminos, honey, fish sauce, ginger, and garlic and process until smooth. Mix in the cilantro. Season with salt and pepper to taste.

5. To make the salad: In a large bowl, combine the cabbage, bell peppers, daikon, cucumber, mango, and green onions. Add the dressing and toss. Slice the steak against the grain and serve over the salad.

VARIATIONS: *Play around with a variety of different vegetables and proteins for this dish—most combinations are delicious.*

NOTE: *As with all cooking, you can always cook something longer, but once you've overcooked something there's no going back. Check the doneness on the steaks a bit before the full time is up, and cook longer if you prefer. Grass-fed beef cooks a bit faster than your standard supermarket cuts. Remember that while your steak rests, the temperature will increase another 5°F.*

STEAK DONENESS CHART

Temperatures are taken before steak has rested.

115–120°F: rare (cool red center)
130–135°F: medium-rare (warm red center)
140–145°F: medium (warm pink center)
150–155°F: medium-well (slightly pink in the middle)
160°F or higher: well done (little or no pink in the meat)

Crispy Prosciutto Salad

Think of this as a minimalist warm bacon dressing salad, with crispy prosciutto taking center stage. Want to make this more of a meal? Add some grilled chicken, steak, or shrimp or some hard-boiled eggs to boost the protein content. Frying the prosciutto won't provide enough fat to get it really crispy, so this is a perfect time to use some reserved bacon grease. Don't have any? Opt for some olive oil instead.

SERVES 4 AS A FIRST COURSE / PREP TIME: 10 MINUTES / TOTAL TIME: 20 MINUTES

2 tablespoons bacon grease

4 ounces prosciutto, very thinly sliced

3 shallots, sliced

One 8-ounce package mushrooms, sliced

2 tablespoons red wine vinegar

1 tablespoon balsamic vinegar

1 teaspoon Dijon mustard

¼ cup olive oil

8 cups baby spinach

1 cup quartered cherry tomatoes (about 1½ cups whole)

1. Heat a large skillet over medium-high heat and add 1 tablespoon of the bacon grease. Add the prosciutto pieces and cook until crispy, about 5 minutes. Remove to a plate and break into small pieces.

2. Add the shallots and mushrooms (see Note) to the pan and sauté until the mushrooms have softened, about 5 minutes.

3. Pour the vinegars and mustard into the pan and stir to incorporate all. Add the remaining 1 tablespoon bacon grease and the olive oil and stir to combine. Keep the dressing warm until ready to dress the salad.

4. Place the spinach and tomatoes in a large bowl and pour the mushroom/shallot/dressing mixture over the spinach, tossing to combine.

5. Serve topped with the prosciutto.

NOTE: *Very typically spinach salads (like what you might find at a restaurant) are served with raw mushrooms. If you prefer your salad that way, don't add the mushrooms to the skillet in step 2 of the instructions, and instead toss the raw mushrooms with the salad in step 4.*

Spicy Lamb Stir-Fry with Mint and Eggplant

Lamb has a particular taste that some people love but that others don't particularly enjoy. Some call it gamey, we call it delicious. If you don't have access to or don't wish to use lamb, then select any meat of your choice—venison, beef, or pork all work well here. You could most certainly use ground beef too, if you want. Serve over cauliflower rice (see "How to Cook Cauliflower Rice," page 30) topped with fresh mint.

SERVES 4 TO 6 / PREP TIME: 10 MINUTES / TOTAL TIME: 25 MINUTES

2 tablespoons fat (coconut oil, olive oil, lard, or ghee)

1½ pounds boneless lamb, cut into 1-inch strips

1 medium red onion, sliced

1 pound eggplant, peeled and cut into ½-inch cubes

2 cloves garlic, minced

2 small Thai chiles, finely chopped (see Note)

2 teaspoons ground turmeric

1 tablespoon ground cumin

1 teaspoon ground cinnamon

1 cup full-fat coconut milk

2 tablespoons minced fresh mint, plus more for serving

1 tablespoon fresh Italian (flat-leaf) parsley, chopped

1. Heat a large Dutch oven over medium-high heat. Add the fat and when shimmering, add the lamb and sauté until browned, about 3 to 5 minutes. Remove to a plate.

2. Reduce the heat to medium, add the onion to the pan, and stir, scraping up any of the browned bits on the bottom of the pan. Add the eggplant and garlic and sauté until the garlic is fragrant and the onion translucent, about 3 more minutes.

3. Stir in the chiles, turmeric, cumin, cinnamon, coconut milk, mint, and parsley. Increase the heat to medium-high and return the lamb to the pot. Cook until the eggplant is softened and the flavors well combined, 5 to 7 minutes.

NOTE: *Thai chiles are pretty fiery. Actually, they're very fiery. If you shy away from spicy things, omit them while cooking and only add in after you've tasted the dish and can determine how much, if any, you want to add to increase the spice level.*

Cucumber and Seafood Salad

This salad dates back some twenty years or so, to when my friend Jonn was making this as part of his signature dish at Druid Hills Golf Club. He included wakame—a Japanese seaweed salad—that really added something special. Most of the store-bought wakame salads I've found at Asian grocers or in the Asian section of your local grocery store have a lot of artificial additives; but if you can find one that doesn't, by all means include it, as seaweed is a great source of naturally occurring iodine. **—JULIE**

SERVES 3 OR 4 AS A SIDE DISH / PREP TIME: 10 MINUTES / TOTAL TIME: 25 MINUTES

1 English cucumber, seeded and sliced on an angle into long slices (see Note)

1 small daikon, thinly sliced

1 carrot, julienned or sliced

2 teaspoons salt

½ cup wakame salad (optional)

¼ red onion, thinly sliced

2 tablespoons unseasoned rice vinegar

½ teaspoon sesame oil

1 tablespoon fresh lemon juice

2 teaspoons honey

¼ pound cooked shrimp or crabmeat, coarsely chopped

1. In a large bowl, combine the cucumber, daikon, and carrot and toss with the salt. Allow to marinate for 10 minutes, then place in a colander, rinse, and drain and return to the bowl.

2. Add the wakame (if using), onion, vinegar, sesame oil, lemon juice, and honey to the vegetables and stir to combine.

3. Stir in the shrimp or crabmeat and keep refrigerated until ready to eat.

NOTE: *This is one of those recipes where a mandoline slicer comes in really handy and makes for very quick prep work!*

Fish Burgers with Wasabi

There's a reason you'll find wasabi accompanying your sashimi or sushi platter. For starters, wasabi's kick helps neutralize the "fishiness" of that nice piece of toro or hamachi, and it's a perfect complement too. It's thought that it also has some antimicrobial properties and might actually prevent food poisoning—some pretty compelling reasons to like the stuff! Here's what you might not know: Though lots of things are labeled "wasabi," true, raw, authentic wasabi is really hard to come by— and really expensive. Most of the time what we are eating is regular (not Japanese) horseradish, usually mixed with mustard, which is a fine substitute and much more accessible and affordable than real wasabi.

SERVES 2 TO 3 / PREP TIME: 5 MINUTES / TOTAL TIME: 20 MINUTES

1 tablespoon coconut aminos

½ teaspoon fish sauce

1 tablespoon wasabi powder

Two 5-ounce cans tuna or salmon, drained, or 10 ounces cooked fish fillets, skinned and finely chopped

1 egg, whisked

1 tablespoon finely minced fresh ginger

1 teaspoon sesame oil

2 green onions, white and green parts, chopped

1 tablespoon coconut oil or avocado oil

Sauces for dipping

1. In a medium bowl, combine the aminos, fish sauce, and wasabi powder. Add the tuna, egg, ginger, sesame oil, and green onions and mix everything together (we prefer to use our hands to really incorporate things). Form into 6 patties.

2. Heat a large skillet over medium-high heat. Add the oil and when shimmering, add the patties and cook until cooked through, 3 to 4 minutes per side. If you're using fresh fish, the cooking time may be a bit longer.

3. Serve plain or with the sauces of your choice.

NOTE: *Wasabi-O, Eden Foods, and Sushi Sonic (many available on Amazon or Thrive Market) and Penzeys brand have pretty decent ingredients as opposed to some of the others we've seen (which include cornstarch, FD&C yellow, artificial flavors, etc.).*

Olive-Crusted Flounder

Ever since our second book, *Quick & Easy Paleo Comfort Foods*, came out, we've been experimenting with pork rinds, as they provide great flavor and texture. The combination of briny, crunchy, and flaky in this recipe will have your mouth watering for more. Served with a light slaw or green salad this makes a perfect meal. I also look forward to our trips to Mobile, Alabama, so that we can make this with fresh-caught flounder or trout.

—CHARLES

SERVES 4 TO 6 / PREP TIME: 10 MINUTES / TOTAL TIME: 25 MINUTES

½ cup black olives, coarsely chopped

2 ounces pork rinds, coarsely ground (see Notes)

1 tablespoon chopped fresh tarragon

1 clove garlic, chopped

¼ cup chopped green onion

2 tablespoons ghee, softened

1½ pounds flounder fillets, skin-on or skinless (see Notes)

1 lime, quartered

1. Preheat the oven to 450°F.
2. Line a baking sheet with parchment paper.
3. In a medium bowl, combine the olives, pork rinds, tarragon, garlic, green onion, and ghee and combine well.
4. Pat fillets dry with a paper towel. Place the fillets on the lined baking sheet (skin side down if they're skin-on). Spoon the olive mixture evenly on top of the fillets, pressing down lightly to cover the fish.
5. Bake until the crust is golden brown, 10 to 15 minutes.
6. Serve immediately with a squeeze of lime juice.

NOTES: *One quick way to grind up the pork rinds is to leave them in the bag and crush them down to a coarse powder. Seal any leftover rinds in a resealable bag to keep fresh.*

Any flaky white fish will do if you don't have flounder handy.

Sloppy Joes

You know you have a winner meal plan when it involves the dish being immortalized in a song by Adam Sandler. This was one of my favorite dishes when I was growing up, though back then I certainly didn't have an appreciation for the little complexities a recipe like this offers. Most of my Sloppy Joe experiences were in the elementary school cafeteria, and I'm guessing that several of the stain-removal products used today were born out of post–Sloppy Joe day at school.

—CHARLES

SERVES 3 TO 4 / PREP TIME: 5 MINUTES / TOTAL TIME: 20 MINUTES

1 tablespoon coconut oil or lard

1 small onion, diced

1 pound ground beef

One 6-ounce can tomato paste

1 tablespoon brown or yellow mustard

½ cup beef stock

1 tablespoon apple cider vinegar

½ teaspoon liquid smoke

2 teaspoons garlic powder

1 teaspoon chili powder

Salt and black pepper

Endive, Bibb, or romaine lettuce, for serving

1. In large skillet, heat the oil over medium-high heat. Add the onion and sauté 2 to 3 minutes or until slightly translucent.

2. Add the beef and cook for 6 to 8 minutes, until browned. Use a wooden spoon to break up the meat into small bits as it cooks.

3. Add the tomato paste, mustard, stock, vinegar, liquid smoke, garlic powder, and chili powder, stirring very thoroughly to combine well. Season with salt and pepper to taste. Continue cooking for 5 to 10 minutes to thicken the sauce somewhat and give the flavors a chance to meld.

4. Serve in endive or Bibb or romaine lettuce leaves. You can also serve a scoop on a bed of greens.

NOTES: *Double this recipe and make extra for the rest of your week. This recipe can be repurposed for breakfast skillets, salad toppings, and stuffing peppers. It also makes a fun appetizer by spooning a dollop onto cucumber slices.*

Pan-Seared Frozen Steaks with Spinach-Artichoke Dip

Get ready for your world to be rocked. This recipe lets your steak go right from frozen to fabulous, and with an accompaniment that's sure to please. Thanks to the kind folks at America's Test Kitchen and Modernist Cuisine for their efforts in showing that frozen steaks are even better than thawed ones!

SERVES 6 TO 8 / PREP TIME: 10 MINUTES / TOTAL TIME: 40 MINUTES

2 tablespoons fat (lard, coconut oil, ghee, or butter)

Two 1-pound steaks of your choice (rib-eye, Porterhouse, and T-bone all work great), cut to even thickness (see Notes)

Salt and black pepper

FOR THE DIP

1 tablespoon fat (ghee, butter, or coconut oil)

2 cloves garlic, minced

½ onion, minced

1 teaspoon arrowroot starch/flour or tapioca flour

1 cup full-fat coconut milk or heavy cream

1 cup grated Parmesan cheese (optional)

10 ounces frozen spinach or 8 cups fresh (don't worry, it cooks down!)

One 14-ounce can artichoke hearts, coarsely chopped

1 teaspoon fresh lemon juice

Dash hot sauce (optional)

1 teaspoon sweet paprika

Salt and black pepper

1. Preheat the oven to 275°F. Place a wire rack on a rimmed baking sheet.

2. Heat a large skillet over high heat. When hot, add the fat, and once simmering, add the steaks (one at a time if need be) and sear until golden brown, pressing down on the steak to ensure that it gets evenly browned. Flip the steaks, sear for a minute or two more, then place on the wire rack. Place in the oven and cook until an instant-read thermometer registers 5°F shy of the internal temperature you desire (in our case, 130°F for medium-rare), 18 to 20 minutes.

3. Tent the steak with foil and allow to rest for 5 to 10 minutes before slicing. Season with salt and pepper.

4. Meanwhile, to make the dip: In a large skillet or saucepan, melt the fat over medium heat. Add the garlic and onion and sauté until the onion is softened, 1 to 2 minutes. Mix in the arrowroot starch/flour and stir to combine.

(recipe continues)

(continued from previous page)

5. Whisk in the coconut milk and continue cooking over medium heat 1 to 2 minutes longer, until the mixture has started to thicken.

6. Stir in the Parmesan (if using), spinach, artichoke hearts, lemon juice, hot sauce (if using), and paprika. Cook for 3 to 4 minutes to heat through (if using fresh spinach, you may need to increase the cooking time to allow the spinach to fully wilt). Taste and season with salt and pepper.

7. Serve the dip alongside or on top of the steaks.

NOTES: *In order to get a good sear on your steak, you will want to use steaks that have been frozen flat; if they're curved, you will have parts of your steak in contact with the skillet when other parts are not. If you have a raw steak at the ready, you can freeze for 30 to 60 minutes before proceeding as above, though you will most likely need to decrease the oven cooking time.*

Eggs Colorado

There's this notion that eggs can or should only be for breakfast. We disagree—especially when adding a few eggs to some leftovers can stretch a meal and keep us full and satisfied. Besides, they are one of the quickest cooking, least expensive protein choices available, and full of choline to boot. We wish we could come up with a fun name like "Shakshuka" or "Eggs in Purgatory" for this, as they are so fun to say. At the risk of you envisioning your eggs donning ski apparel or flannel shirts and hiking boots, we'll remind you that Colorado in this sense simply means "red" (sauce).

SERVES 3 TO 4 / PREP TIME: 5 MINUTES / TOTAL TIME: 15 MINUTES

2 cups Chile Colorado (page 74) or any other chili you have on hand

1 cup canned crushed tomatoes or your favorite tomato sauce

6 large eggs

¼ cup fresh cilantro leaves, minced

1 avocado, diced

1. In a large skillet, bring the chile colorado and tomatoes to a simmer over medium heat.
2. Make 6 indentations in the sauce and crack an egg into each of the indentations.
3. Reduce the heat to low, cover, and cook until the egg yolks are just set but still runny, 6 to 8 minutes.
4. Serve with the cilantro and avocado.

VARIATION: *If you prefer a meatless version or you don't have chili on hand, simply use 3 cups total of tomato sauce (like our 5-Ingredient Tomato Sauce on page 214).*

Pancetta-Wrapped Cod

This is a light and extremely flavorful recipe that was born of my short stint living in a small kitchenless apartment in Atlanta. I managed to bring a hot plate and griddle with me and recipes like this were a lifesaver. Not only is it quick and tasty, it doesn't require much in the way of equipment.

—CHARLES

SERVES 4 TO 6 / PREP TIME: 10 MINUTES / TOTAL TIME: 25 MINUTES

6 cod fillets

6 very thin slices pancetta or prosciutto

2 tablespoons lard

¼ cup capers, rinsed and well drained

Juice of 2 lemons

2 tablespoons olive oil

Black pepper

2 tablespoons coarsely chopped fresh Italian (flat-leaf) parsley

1. Pat the fillets dry. Wrap the pancetta around the fish and secure with a toothpick.

2. In a large skillet, heat the lard over medium-high heat. Add the fillets and sear for several minutes on each side. Turn them carefully so the fish doesn't fall apart. Reduce the heat to low and continue cooking until the fish flakes easily, 2 to 3 minutes.

3. In a small saucepan, combine the capers, lemon juice, and olive oil. Crack some pepper over the mixture and bring to a simmer over medium heat, stirring occasionally.

4. Serve the fish with the caper sauce and garnish with the parsley.

NOTE: *This recipe pairs very well with freshly cooked vegetables or a salad.*

Philly-Style Steak with Onions and Mushrooms

As my family lived (and still lives) about 45 minutes outside of Philadelphia, we never got into the whole Pat's vs. Geno's cheesesteak debate. No, our cheesesteak consumption was probably 95 percent homemade ones. Hold on, let me stop right there before you get too excited: This is not, nor should it be thought of as, a "Paleo cheesesteak." Let me make this doubly clear: This is not trying to be a "Paleo cheesesteak" on a lettuce wrap. For starters, there's no cheese (though if you do dairy and want to add cheese, go for it; see Note)! However, this is reminiscent of when my mom would make us cheesesteaks growing up. The aroma of the sautéed onions and mushrooms, and the so-thinly-sliced beef that would get a little crispy from being cooked in the skillet, bring back so many fond memories. Besides, it's hard to go wrong with steak sautéed with mushrooms and onions anyway. The key to this dish is slicing your beef as thinly as is humanly possible. Charles once said he'd love a meat slicer, and recipes like this one have me almost considering it.

—JULIE

SERVES 3 TO 4 / PREP TIME: 15 MINUTES / TOTAL TIME: 25 MINUTES

1 tablespoon fat (butter, ghee, or coconut oil)

1 yellow onion, thinly sliced

2 cups white mushrooms, sliced

1 pound top sirloin, rib-eye, or skirt steak, sliced as thin as possible

½ teaspoon salt

½ teaspoon black pepper

Romaine or other lettuce leaves, for serving

1. Heat a large skillet over medium-high heat. Add the fat and once hot, add the onion and mushrooms and sauté until golden brown and slightly caramelized, 6 to 7 minutes. Move to one side of the pan.

2. Add the steak and break apart any large chunks to have as much of the meat in contact with the skillet as possible. Sauté until the meat is cooked through, seasoning with the salt and pepper. Add more fat if the meat looks too dry.

3. Serve on lettuce leaves.

NOTE: *In Philly there's this whole debate about whether to use Cheez Whiz or provolone on a cheese steak. If you're going to add cheese to this recipe, provolone is a much better option in my book.*

Spiced Pork Skillet

One of my favorite meals growing up was "breakfast dinner." Traditionally, this was scrambled eggs and bacon or sausage and grits. As the flavors of this one are much like those you'd find in a breakfast sausage, it brings back memories of those breakfast dinners. This is a great eggless recipe to keep variety in your morning chow or it's a great quick dinner solution at night. Leftovers heat up very easily and can be repurposed for another meal.

—CHARLES

SERVES 3 TO 4 / PREP TIME: 5 MINUTES / TOTAL TIME: 20 MINUTES

1 pound ground pork (see Notes)

1 teaspoon sea salt

½ teaspoon black pepper

½ teaspoon dried marjoram

½ teaspoon dried thyme

¼ teaspoon rubbed sage

¼ teaspoon dried oregano

2 tablespoons butter

1 cup diced onion

3 cloves garlic, minced

2 medium apples, cored and diced

½ teaspoon ground cinnamon

1. In a large skillet, brown the pork over medium heat. Use a wooden spoon to break up the pork into small bits as it cooks. Add the salt, pepper, marjoram, thyme, sage, and oregano, stirring to combine well. Remove the pork from the skillet and set aside.

2. Add the butter to the skillet and sauté the onions and garlic over medium heat until the onions soften, 3 to 5 minutes.

3. Add the apples and cinnamon, then return the pork to the skillet, stirring to combine. Cover and simmer for about 2 minutes to soften the apples. Serve hot.

NOTES: *Double or triple this recipe to feed a hungry crowd.*

If you have a local resource that makes a bulk sausage with good ingredients, feel free to use that as a substitute for the ground pork and spices to save a little time.

SAUCES AND STAPLES

We suppose you could call this chapter "how to make a bunch of usually store-bought things at home." These recipes are much cleaner than what you might find on store shelves, and enable you to control ingredients much more to your personal desires. Here are some of our favorites to share with you.

Chicken Stock	209
Basic Mayonnaise	211
Honey-Mustard Sauce	212
Sriracha-Sesame Mayonnaise	212
Lime Mayonnaise	212
Rosemary-Garlic Mayonnaise	213
5-Ingredient Tomato Sauce	214
Avocado Sauce	215
No-Cook Barbecue Sauce	216
Pico de Gallo (Salsa Fresca)	218
Salsa Verde	219
Roasty Toasty Pepper Dip	220
Spice Blends	221
Baharat Seasoning	221
Moroccan Spice Blend	222
Steak Seasoning	223
Dukkah	224
Fajita Seasoning	224
Cajun Spice Mix	225
Chili Powder	225
Chipotle Sauce	227
Magic Nut Butter	228

Chicken Stock

Julie has a knack for getting me some rather amazing presents. There was that year when I spent a day butchering a pig and making bacon with Pine Street Market. Then another time when I got to go hog hunting in Texas with my buddies Robb, John, Dave, and a bunch of guys to support the Silent Warrior Scholarship Fund. Those were all pretty amazing, but she may have topped them all with a recent Christmas gift. Four days before the event, I got a text from her saying "You should go to this." It was an event about holistic resource management featuring the ecologist Allan Savory being held at White Oak Pastures—the largest USDA Certified Organic farm in Georgia and the only farm in the United States with both chicken and beef abbatoir on the premises. Spending two days with Savory and the incomparable Will Harris (whose family has owned White Oak Pastures for the last 150 years) was transformative for me. Before leaving the farm, I made sure to stop in the country store and buy some chicken feet. It was finally time for me to buck up and make the most epic of chicken stocks ever.

—CHARLES

MAKES 3 QUARTS / PREP TIME: 15 MINUTES / TOTAL TIME: 8 TO 16 HOURS

3 ribs celery with leaves, coarsely chopped

2 carrots, coarsely chopped

1 large onion, quartered

3 cloves garlic

1 tablespoon olive oil

2½ pounds chicken feet or the carcass from a whole chicken

3 quarts spring water

1. Position the rack about 3 inches away from the heating element and preheat the broiler to 450°F. Line a baking sheet with foil.

2. In a bowl, toss the celery, carrots, onion, and garlic with the olive oil. Spread the vegetables on the baking sheet. Broil for 10 minutes, turning once after 5 minutes.

3. Dump the roasted veggies into a slow cooker. Add the chicken feet and water. Cover and cook on low for 8 hours or more (see Note).

4. When done, strain the stock through cheesecloth or a fine-mesh sieve. Use immediately or pour into containers for storage. The stock freezes well for 4 to 6 months.

NOTE: *This stock gets better the longer it cooks. I sometimes run the slow cooker through two 8-hour cycles, or I strain the first batch off after the first cycle and dump another 3 quarts of water in for another batch.*

Basic Mayonnaise (with variations)

Why not just stick to store-bought mayonnaise? Typically, most are made with soybean or canola oils, and these and other vegetable-based, highly refined oils like them are high in polyunsaturated fats and omega-6 fatty acids, extremely prone to oxidation and very often processed with chemicals you don't want or need in your food. While some resources still tout these as so-called healthy oils, more and more research seems to be indicating that polyunsaturated fats are far more problematic than saturated fats. Our great-grandparents lived in an age when vegetable-based oils like corn and canola and soybean oil were pretty much nonexistent. In our opinion, steering clear of these heavily processed, ultrarefined oils makes a ton of sense. And besides: It's so very easy to make your own mayonnaise!

The Basic Mayonnaise and all variations will keep for up to 1 week in the refrigerator.

MAKES 1 CUP / PREP TIME: 5 MINUTES / TOTAL TIME: 10 MINUTES

1 large egg, at room temperature

1 tablespoon fresh lemon juice

1 tablespoon apple cider vinegar

½ teaspoon mustard powder

½ teaspoon sea salt

1 cup avocado oil or macadamia nut oil

Food processor method:
In a food processor, combine the egg, lemon juice, vinegar, mustard powder, and salt. Process until the mixture turns a pale yellow. With the machine running, very slowly drizzle in the oil until the mayo thickens and emulsifies.

Immersion blender method:
The steps are relatively the same. In the cup that came with your immersion blender (or a jar or other receptacle that the blender fits into snugly), combine the egg, lemon juice, vinegar, mustard powder, and salt and pulse a few times to blend. Slowly add the oil, making sure everything is well blended before adding more. For a thicker mayo, add more oil.

NOTES: *If the mayonnaise breaks (i.e., gets all clumpy or oily-looking), all hope is not lost! In a bowl, whisk another room temperature egg yolk until it's pale yellow. Then, using a whisk or immersion blender, slowly start to add the broken mayonnaise to the yolk.*

Honey-Mustard Sauce

Sure to be a winner with the kids—especially when paired with our chicken nuggets (page 47).

½ cup mayonnaise, store-bought or homemade (page 211)

2 tablespoons yellow mustard

1 tablespoon Dijon mustard

1 to 2 tablespoons honey (to taste)

2 teaspoons fresh lemon juice

In a bowl, stir together the mayonnaise, mustards, honey, and lemon juice. Keep refrigerated until ready to serve.

Sriracha-Sesame Mayonnaise

This is a favorite burger topper for us!

½ cup mayonnaise, store-bought or homemade (page 211)

2 to 3 teaspoons Sriracha sauce (to taste)

1 teaspoon sesame oil

In a bowl, stir together the mayonnaise, Sriracha, and sesame oil. Keep refrigerated until ready to use.

Lime Mayonnaise

A great one to serve on top of fish, as a dip for Chicken Nuggets Redux (page 47), drizzled over a sweet potato, or served alongside some Plantain Chips (page 240).

½ cup mayonnaise, store-bought or homemade (page 211)

1 teaspoon fresh lime juice

1 teaspoon distilled white vinegar

In a bowl, stir together the mayonnaise, lime juice, and vinegar. Keep refrigerated until ready to use.

Rosemary-Garlic Mayonnaise

This is so incredibly tasty served on top of steak or a grilled pork chop!

½ cup mayonnaise, store-bought or homemade (page 211)

1 tablespoon fresh rosemary, minced

1 clove garlic, minced

Pinch of salt

In a bowl, stir together the mayonnaise, rosemary, garlic, and salt. Keep refrigerated until ready to use.

A NOTE ABOUT EGG SAFETY

Some folks get really worried about the risk of salmonella and uncooked eggs. Home pasteurization of eggs is relatively easy, though there is no guarantee that the pasteurization will absolutely kill off any potential harmful bacteria. First line of defense is definitely to buy your eggs from a trusted, reliable source! Should you wish to home pasteurize: Let the eggs come to room temperature. Place them in a pot and cover them with cold water (there should be at least an inch of water above the eggs). Have your instant-read thermometer handy. Heat the pan over medium heat until the water reaches 140°F (going above 150°F will change the texture of the eggs). Once the thermometer registers 140°F, maintain that temperature for 3 to 5 minutes. Remove the eggs from the hot water and rinse under cold water.

5-Ingredient Tomato Sauce

You can find decent—even really good—tomato sauce in the store these days, but there's always something special about homemade. While this sauce is technically ready in minutes, the flavors intensify the longer you let it simmer. This is a very simple recipe, and the tomatoes you choose will make all the difference. Our preference is for home-canned (peeled) tomatoes, followed by canned whole, peeled San Marzano tomatoes. Oh, and yes, we realize that there are actually 7 ingredients listed here. Do we really have to count salt and pepper?

MAKES ABOUT 7 CUPS / PREP TIME: 5 MINUTES / TOTAL TIME: 30 MINUTES TO 1 HOUR

1 tablespoon plus ¼ cup extra-virgin olive oil

1 sweet onion, minced

2 tablespoons minced garlic (4 to 6 large cloves)

Two 28-ounce cans tomatoes

½ cup fresh basil, shredded

½ teaspoon salt

¼ teaspoon black pepper

1. In a Dutch oven or large pot, heat 1 tablespoon of the olive oil over medium heat. When hot, add the onion and sauté until translucent, about 5 minutes. Stir in the garlic and sauté a minute more.

2. Mix in the tomatoes, crushing with a wooden spoon or spatula in the pot, and simmer over medium-low heat until the sauce begins to darken and thicken, at least 20 minutes but ideally for 1 hour.

3. Add the basil, remaining ¼ cup olive oil, salt, and pepper.

Slow cooker method:
In a skillet, sauté the onion and garlic in 1 tablespoon oil as directed in the recipe. Add the onion, garlic, and tomatoes to a slow cooker and cook on low for 6 to 8 hours. Stir in the basil, ¼ cup oil, salt, and pepper.

Pressure cooker method:
In a pressure cooker, sauté the onion and garlic in 1 tablespoon oil as directed in the recipe. (If using an Instant Pot, select the sauté feature.) Mix in the tomatoes. Seal and cook for 15 minutes at high pressure. Use the quick-release for the pressure, then stir in the basil, ¼ cup oil, salt, and pepper.

Avocado Sauce

This is not guacamole—we promise. Rather, here's a lovely thin green sauce that is perfect on so many dishes or even as a salad dressing, served atop Carnitas (page 73) or drizzled over your favorite piece of fish.

MAKES ABOUT ¾ CUP / PREP TIME: 5 MINUTES / TOTAL TIME: 10 MINUTES

1 avocado, pitted and peeled

1 to 2 teaspoons water, coconut milk, or almond milk

1 teaspoon fresh lime juice

½ teaspoon ground cumin

Dash of salt

2 teaspoons chopped fresh cilantro

In a small food processor or blender, combine the avocado, 1 teaspoon of the water, the lime juice, cumin, and salt and puree until smooth. Stir in the cilantro and adjust the seasoning as you see fit. For a thinner sauce, add more liquid.

No-Cook Barbecue Sauce

Tinkering with this recipe was fun. I'm a long-standing fan of cooked barbecue sauces and wasn't sure how much goodness I could concoct without firing up the stovetop. It took a few tries and I think you'll agree this is a keeper. Barbecue sauce can add a deep and complex flavor to leftovers. Adding a dollop to a soup or stew is a great way to change up the taste in a subtle way. —CHARLES

MAKES ABOUT 2 CUPS / PREP TIME: UNDER 10 MINUTES / TOTAL TIME: UNDER 10 MINUTES

1 cup canned fire-roasted tomatoes

¼ cup apple cider vinegar

4 dates, pitted

2 tablespoons coconut aminos

2 tablespoons tomato paste

2 tablespoons Dijon mustard

1 teaspoon liquid smoke

1 tablespoon garlic powder

2 teaspoons sea salt

1 teaspoon black pepper

½ teaspoon cayenne pepper

½ teaspoon crushed red pepper

In a food processor, combine all the ingredients and process until smooth. Use immediately or refrigerate. The barbecue sauce will keep for at least 2 weeks in the refrigerator.

Pico de Gallo (Salsa Fresca)

What's the difference between pico de gallo and salsa? Technically, pico de gallo is never cooked, and usually has chunks of the vegetables, whereas salsa can be cooked or raw, chunky or smooth, canned or fresh, and can contain ingredients other than the ones listed below. Our personal preference is to make pico de gallo, because it's super easy to mix in with some mashed avocado and have a variation of a quick guacamole (though guacamole purists will insist that tomatoes are not a part of that recipe). Either way, this is one of our all-time favorite salad dressings and it's perfect over Carnitas (page 73).　　**—JULIE**

MAKES 2 TO 2½ CUPS　/　PREP TIME: 10 MINUTES　/　TOTAL TIME: 20 MINUTES, PLUS STANDING TIME (FOR THE FLAVORS TO MELD)

1 pound tomatoes, seeded and diced

1 teaspoon sea salt

½ red or white onion, diced

1 serrano or jalapeño pepper, diced (seeding optional; remove if you want things a bit milder)

¼ cup chopped fresh cilantro

Juice of ½ lime (about 1 tablespoon), or more to taste

1. In a large bowl, combine the tomatoes and sea salt and let sit for about 10 minutes.

2. Mix in the onion, chile pepper, cilantro, and lime juice and stir well, allowing the flavors to marry for at least 10 minutes before serving.

NOTE: *I think the salting of the tomatoes really makes a difference in the flavors here!*

Salsa Verde

Need a quick way to dress up some eggs? Try this salsa verde. Want a dip that you can bring to a friend's house that is not guacamole? Give this a go. Want the perfect accompaniment for our Green Enchiladas (page 36)? This is it!

MAKES 2 TO 2½ CUPS / PREP TIME: 10 MINUTES / TOTAL TIME: 15 MINUTES

1 pound tomatillos, husked and rinsed (see Notes)

1 small onion, cut into large chunks

2 cloves garlic, peeled

2 jalapeño peppers, coarsely chopped

Juice of 1 lime

½ cup fresh cilantro (leaves and stems)

Salt to taste

1. In a food processor or blender, combine the tomatillos, onion, garlic, peppers, lime juice, cilantro, and salt and blend to desired consistency.

2. Pour the salsa into a nonreactive saucepan and bring to a boil. Reduce the heat and simmer for 10 minutes.

NOTES: *For a slightly charred flavor, roast or broil the tomatillos and onions first*

If you cannot find fresh tomatillos, use canned, but be sure to drain off the liquid.

Roasty Toasty Pepper Dip

Serve with homemade crackers or cut vegetables as an appetizer.

MAKES 1½ CUPS / PREP TIME: 5 MINUTES / TOTAL TIME: 10 MINUTES

1 cup raw or roasted cashews

½ cup jarred roasted red peppers

2 cloves garlic, peeled

½ cup chicken stock or water

1 teaspoon sea salt

¼ teaspoon sweet paprika

¼ teaspoon chipotle powder

1. If using raw cashews, toast them in a skillet over medium-high heat until they are fragrant and browned.

2. Add the cashews to a food processor and grind into a coarse butter. Add the roasted peppers, garlic, chicken stock, salt, paprika, and chipotle powder. Process until creamy smooth.

3. Serve immediately or store in the refrigerator for up to 1 week.

VARIATION: *For a delicious and quick dinner, add a bit more stock to this recipe and pour the sauce over chicken pieces. Bake at 375°F for 15 to 20 minutes.*

Spice Blends

There's the old saying that "variety is the spice of life," but we like to think that spices are the variety of life too, at least when it comes to the kitchen. While there are some great off-the-shelf spice blends you can purchase, many have additives and sugars, where others already have salt in them, which makes it difficult to control for your own tastes and liking. Here are some blends we keep on hand.

Baharat Seasoning

This Middle Eastern spice blend is a sure way to spice up any meat, whether grilling, braising, or frying. Add a few teaspoons to soups to give them a nice flare too.

MAKES ABOUT ½ CUP / TOTAL TIME: 5 MINUTES

1 tablespoon black peppercorns

1 tablespoon coriander seeds

1 tablespoon cumin seeds

2 teaspoons cardamom seeds

2 teaspoons allspice berries

½ teaspoon whole cloves

1 cinnamon stick

1 tablespoon sweet paprika

2 teaspoons ground turmeric

¼ teaspoon ground nutmeg

1. Heat a small skillet over medium heat. Add the peppercorns, coriander seeds, cumin seeds, cardamom seeds, allspice berries, and cloves and toast for 2 to 3 minutes, stirring constantly, until fragrant.

2. Place the toasted spices in a spice grinder along with the cinnamon stick and grind thoroughly.

3. Add the paprika, turmeric, and nutmeg and combine thoroughly.

4. Store in a glass or metal shaker or resealable plastic bag for future use.

Moroccan Spice Blend

Eleanor's Wings were a huge hit in our second book, *Quick & Easy Paleo Comfort Foods*. This spice blend is reminiscent of the mixture we used in that recipe, and can add incredible depth and flavor to any dish.

MAKES ABOUT ¼ CUP / TOTAL TIME: 5 MINUTES

1 tablespoon cumin seeds

2 teaspoons coriander seeds

1 teaspoon whole cloves

1 tablespoon ground ginger

2 teaspoons ground cinnamon

2 teaspoons salt

1 teaspoon ground allspice

1 teaspoon black pepper

1 teaspoon cayenne pepper

1 teaspoon ground turmeric

1. Heat a small skillet over medium heat. Add the cumin seeds, coriander seeds, and cloves and toast until fragrant, tossing frequently, for 2 to 3 minutes.

2. Place the toasted spices in a spice grinder and grind thoroughly. Add the ground ginger, cinnamon, salt, allspice, black pepper, cayenne, and turmeric and blend in.

3. Store in a glass or metal shaker or resealable plastic bag for future use.

Steak Seasoning

Dad's Famous Rub from our first book was incredibly popular, the recipe being a take on my dad's extremely popular rib rub. This steak seasoning pays its respects to the former, with a few unexpected flavorings (like dill) to change up things a bit. Don't let the name fool you, though, as this recipe is great over any fish, in any stew, even sprinkled on roasted vegetables. If you choose to include the crushed red pepper, just know that it does lean heavily toward the "fiery" side—in other words, prepare to experience a day in the life of my taste buds.

—CHARLES

MAKES JUST OVER ½ CUP / TOTAL TIME: UNDER 5 MINUTES

2 tablespoons kosher salt

1 tablespoon ancho powder

1 tablespoon black pepper

1 tablespoon sweet paprika

1 tablespoon garlic powder

1 tablespoon onion powder

1 tablespoon dried dill seed

1 tablespoon dried oregano

1 tablespoon crushed red pepper (optional)

In a bowl or shaker, combine all the ingredients. Store in a glass or metal shaker or resealable plastic bag for future use.

Dukkah

This Egyptian spice blend contains a combination of herbs, nuts, and seeds. It has evolved many times over its history. We love having this on hand when it's time to cook some meat.

MAKES ABOUT ½ CUP / TOTAL TIME: 10 MINUTES

¼ cup macadamia nuts

1 tablespoon sesame seeds

1 tablespoon coriander seeds

1 tablespoon cumin seeds

¼ teaspoon black peppercorns

2 teaspoons dried marjoram

1 teaspoon sea salt

½ teaspoon crushed red pepper

1. In a small skillet, toast the macadamia nuts and sesame seeds over medium heat until fragrant. Remove from the pan to cool.

2. In the same pan, toast the coriander seeds, cumin seeds, and black peppercorns until fragrant. Remove from the pan to cool.

3. Once all the ingredients are cooled, combine them and the remaining ingredients in a small food processor and pulse to the consistency you desire. Be careful not to overgrind or the mixture will turn into a paste. Store in the refrigerator for up to a month.

Fajita Seasoning

The is one of our favorite all-purpose seasonings. It can be used on everything from eggs to broccoli.

MAKES ¼ CUP PLUS ½ TEASPOON / TOTAL TIME: UNDER 5 MINUTES

2 tablespoons chili powder

2 teaspoons garlic powder

1½ teaspoons ground cumin

½ teaspoon onion powder

½ teaspoon dried oregano

½ teaspoon sweet paprika

1 teaspoon salt

½ teaspoon black pepper

In a small bowl, combine all the spices.

Cajun Spice Mix

This bayou seasoning adds just the right spark to nearly any meal. It adds so much flavor to seafood, vegetables, and even the occasional burger. This blend will have your taste buds grateful you took a few minutes to mix it up.

MAKES JUST OVER ½ CUP / TOTAL TIME: UNDER 10 MINUTES

2 tablespoons sea salt

2 tablespoons smoked paprika

1 tablespoon black pepper

1 tablespoon cayenne pepper

1 tablespoon garlic powder

1 tablespoon onion powder

1 tablespoon dried oregano

1 tablespoon dried thyme

2 teaspoons dried basil

2 teaspoons white pepper

In a bowl or shaker, combine all the ingredients. Store in a glass or metal shaker or resealable plastic bag for future use.

Chili Powder

Off-the-shelf chili powder certainly gets the job done, but a homemade spice blend takes things to a different level. You'll love the complexity this blend adds to your stews and meats.

MAKES ABOUT ¼ CUP / TOTAL TIME: UNDER 5 MINUTES

2 tablespoons sweet paprika

2 teaspoons ground cumin

2 teaspoons garlic powder

2 teaspoons mustard powder

1 teaspoon cayenne pepper

1 teaspoon chipotle powder

1 teaspoon onion powder

1 teaspoon dried oregano

In a bowl or shaker, combine all the ingredients. Store in a glass or metal shaker or resealable plastic bag for future use.

Chipotle Sauce

We aren't sure how we survived before chipotle sauce. In recent years (or at least that's our perception), the smoky spicy condiment has been appearing on menus all over, including a bunch of fast-food joints. The challenge is that some canned chipotles in adobo contain a few potentially problematic ingredients (wheat starch, soybean oil, not to mention most have added sugar). Because we use this condiment a lot, we wanted to create something that is Paleo friendly, doesn't involve ingredients we don't keep on hand, and still packs a punch. Some recipes call for doing the various steps separately (soaking chipotles in one bowl, anchos in another, then cooking things on a stovetop). We needed something simpler, so we came up with this.

MAKES ABOUT 3 CUPS / PREP TIME: 5 MINUTES / TOTAL TIME: 25 MINUTES TO 1 HOUR

8 dried chipotle chiles, rinsed and seeded

2 dried ancho chiles, rinsed and seeded

2 cups hot water

¼ cup apple cider vinegar

¼ cup unseasoned rice vinegar

¼ cup tomato paste

½ small onion, minced

2 dates, pitted and mashed into a paste, or 2 tablespoons honey

4 cloves garlic, peeled and minced

1. In a medium saucepan, combine the dried chiles, boiling water, vinegars, tomato paste, onion, date paste, and garlic. Bring to a simmer and cook over medium-low heat for at least 20 minutes, or a bit longer if you like a thicker sauce.
2. Puree in a blender, food processor, or right in the pan with an immersion blender.

NOTE: *We usually store a small jar of the chipotle sauce in the refrigerator (it keeps for a week or so) and then freeze the remaining sauce in ice cube trays for future use. If you want this recipe to make "chipotles in adobo sauce," instead of chipotle sauce, remove some of the whole chipotles from the saucepan after simmering. Set aside, and puree the remaining saucepan contents as in step 2. Return the chipotles to the sauce and refrigerate to store.*

Magic Nut Butter

When it comes to keeping a couple of kids happy around snack time, there is no greater friend than this recipe. We frequently keep a jar of it on our kitchen counter. It's a healthy fat to go with nearly any vegetable or fruit. It also adds a layer of richness to a curry recipe or sauce in a pinch. You may wish to try dipping Toasted Bark (page 238) in the Magic Nut Butter for an extra tasty dessert.

MAKES 2 CUPS / PREP TIME: 5 MINUTES / TOTAL TIME: 10 MINUTES

1 cup macadamia nuts

½ cup raw cashews (see Notes)

½ cup pecans

1 teaspoon sea salt (optional)

1. Heat a large stainless steel skillet over medium-high heat. Add all the nuts to the pan and toast for 2 to 4 minutes, tossing frequently.

2. Transfer the nuts to a food processor, add the salt, and process for 3 to 5 minutes (or until the mixture reaches the desired consistency).

3. Store in an airtight container at room temperature for up to 2 weeks.

NOTES: *This combination is indeed magical, but feel free to play around with the variety of nuts you use.*

Keep a spatula handy while processing the butter, as the nuts have a tendency to stick to the sides of the processor bowl, especially if they are still warm, and you may need to scrape down the sides of the bowl a few times.

SWEETS
AND
TREATS

On occasion, a treat is in order. We like satisfying our celebratory sweet tooth in the tastiest way possible, while also being mindful of how we react to gluten and too much sugar. These are just a few treats that sometimes grace our table from time to time.

Morning Glory Muffins Revisited   233
Apple Crisps   234
Whipped Coconut Cream   235
Pumpkin Pie-Cakes   236
Toasted Bark   238
Plantain Chips   240
Lemon Curd Bites   243
Flourless Chocolate Mini Cakes   244

Morning Glory Muffins Revisited

In 2011, we attended the inaugural Ancestral Health Symposium in Los Angeles. This was a transformative weekend and it gave us the opportunity to meet a number of amazing people in the ancestral health scene for the first time. Knowing this, Charles baked up a few batches of our Morning Glory Muffins from our first book and brought them on the trip. They were a huge hit and remain one of the more popular recipes from that book. It seemed like a great time to tinker with this recipe to accommodate the growing number of people with nut allergies. The original recipe called for almond flour. Substituting coconut flour can be a tricky business to ensure that you don't end up with hockey pucks, but we think we've nailed it with this recipe. This makes a great snack for the kids.

MAKES 12 MUFFINS / PREP TIME: 20 MINUTES / TOTAL TIME: 30 TO 40 MINUTES

Coconut oil, for the pan

1 cup tapioca flour

½ cup coconut flour

1½ teaspoons ground cinnamon

1 teaspoon ground nutmeg

2 teaspoons baking powder

½ teaspoon salt

4 large eggs

⅓ cup avocado oil

1½ teaspoons vanilla extract

1 cup shredded zucchini

1 cup dried currants

1 apple, peeled, cored, and grated (see Note)

Grated zest and juice of 1 orange

⅓ cup full-fat coconut milk

1. Position a rack in the center of the oven and preheat the oven to 325°F. Grease 12 cups of a muffin tin with coconut oil.

2. In a bowl, combine the tapioca flour, coconut flour, cinnamon, nutmeg, baking powder, and salt.

3. In a separate bowl, whisk together the eggs, avocado oil, and vanilla. When thoroughly combined, fold in the zucchini, currants, apple, orange zest, orange juice, and coconut milk.

4. Fold the egg mixture into the flour mixture, making sure there are no streaks. Spoon the batter into the muffin cups and bake until a toothpick inserted into the center of a muffin comes out clean, 15 to 20 minutes.

5. Allow the muffins to cool in the pan for 8 to 10 minutes and then remove to a rack to finish cooling.

NOTE: *Feel free to tinker with the veggie and fruit ingredients on this to your liking, but be sure to keep the ratios the same. Some common substitutions are carrot for zucchini, raisins for currants, and pear for apple.*

Apple Crisps

I'm not sure when my family started our apple crumb pie tradition for holidays; perhaps thirty or so years ago? The original recipe stemmed from an old Betty Crocker cookbook, with the Crisco-based crust from my hometown's Women's Guild cookbook. I've never been a fan of the crust, both from a labor and taste perspective, and was often the family member who ate all the apples and crumb topping, leaving the crust behind. This recipe ditches the crust altogether, and focuses on the flavors that I love—all while cutting out the refined sugars. Top with Whipped Coconut Cream (opposite).　　—JULIE

SERVES 6 / PREP TIME: 10 MINUTES / TOTAL TIME: 30 MINUTES

FOR THE CRUMB TOPPING

5 tablespoons cold unsalted butter, coconut oil, or palm shortening

¼ cup shredded unsweetened coconut

¼ cup chopped pecans or walnuts (optional)

3 tablespoons tapioca flour

2 tablespoons coconut sugar or other sugar

2 teaspoons ground cinnamon

FOR THE FILLING

4 Granny Smith apples, peeled, cored, and cut into bite-size pieces

Juice of 1 lemon

1 teaspoon ground cinnamon

1. Preheat the oven to 375°F.

2. To make the crumb topping: In a bowl, mash the butter with a fork and combine with the shredded coconut, nuts (if using), tapioca flour, sugar, and cinnamon. It should resemble a coarse meal. Set aside.

3. To make the filling: In a bowl, combine the apple, lemon juice, and cinnamon and toss to coat.

4. Divide the apple slices among 6 small (6-ounce) ramekins (the ramekins may seem to be overflowing with the apples, but they cook down quite a bit). Carefully top with the crumb topping mixture and place on a baking pan (see Note).

5. Bake until the juices from the apples are bubbling and softened, 20 to 25 minutes.

NOTE: *Placing a piece of aluminum foil under the ramekins on the baking sheet will help with the cleanup process should any of the juices from the apples overflow during cooking.*

VARIATION: *Pears, berries, peaches—pretty much any fruit would work well in this recipe.*

Whipped Coconut Cream

This is the perfect substitution for those wanting some whipped cream but without adding dairy.

MAKES ALMOST 2 CUPS / PREP TIME: 5 MINUTES (PLUS REFRIGERATION TIME) /
TOTAL TIME: 5 MINUTES

One 14.5-ounce can full-fat coconut milk
½ teaspoon pure vanilla extract

1 to 2 teaspoons coconut sugar or other sweetener (optional)

1. The night before preparing the whipped cream, place the coconut milk in the refrigerator.

2. When ready to make the cream, invert the can, open the bottom, and pour off the thin, runny liquid. Scrape out all the hard coconut cream into a medium bowl and reserve the runny liquid for another use. Using a handheld mixer or stand mixer, beat the cream over high speed until stiff peaks form, about 5 minutes. Add in the vanilla and sugar (if using) and blend for a minute more. Keep refrigerated until ready to serve.

Pumpkin Pie-Cakes

These are like pumpkin pie filling in cupcake form, but not cakey like a cupcake, if that makes any sense at all. In other words, the best of the pumpkin pie world in a bite-size bit. This recipe is inspired by the Impossible Pumpkin Pie Cupcakes recipe on CakesCottage.com.

MAKES 24 MINI MUFFINS / PREP TIME: 8 MINUTES / TOTAL TIME: 20 TO 25 MINUTES

⅔ cup finely ground almond flour

1½ teaspoons pumpkin pie spice

½ teaspoon baking soda

¼ teaspoon sea salt

1½ cups canned pure pumpkin puree

⅓ cup full-fat coconut milk

¼ cup coconut sugar

2 large eggs

½ teaspoon vanilla extract

Whipped Coconut Cream (page 235) or freshly made whipped cream, for serving

1. Preheat the oven to 350°F. Line 24 cups of a mini muffin tin with liners.

2. In a medium bowl, combine the almond flour, pumpkin pie spice, baking soda, and salt. In a separate large bowl, whisk together the pumpkin puree, coconut milk, sugar, eggs, and vanilla.

3. Add the flour mixture to the pumpkin mixture and mix just until combined.

4. Fill the muffin cups about two-thirds full. Bake until just set around the edges, 12 to 15 minutes. They will be rather soft in the center.

5. Remove the muffins from the pan and let cool on a wire rack. Serve topped with whipped coconut cream.

Toasted Bark

The world is more enjoyable with chocolate in it. We love making a batch of this around holidays and special occasions, like Wednesdays. Some of the most fun comes watching our kids clean the bowl when we're done. Nothing says joy more than a kid with chocolate from head to toe.

SERVES 10 TO 20 / PREP TIME: 10 MINUTES / TOTAL TIME: 20 MINUTES

7 ounces fair trade dark chocolate (70% or more cacao), finely chopped

½ cup pecans, toasted and coarsely chopped

1 teaspoon coarse sea salt flakes

1. Gently melt the chocolate using the microwave or a double boiler (see Notes).

2. Evenly spread the chocolate on a parchment-lined cookie sheet to about ⅛-inch thickness.

3. Sprinkle the pecans to cover the chocolate, followed by sea salt.

4. Place the bark in the refrigerator for 5 to 10 minutes to set.

5. Remove and break apart to serve.

NOTES: *Take your time melting the chocolate. If using a microwave, work in 30-second increments and allow the chocolate to rest between sessions. Heating the chocolate too fast can damage it and it won't set properly.*

Any variety of nuts can be used. Feel free to fold in a little smoked paprika or chipotle powder to the chocolate to give it a kick.

Plantain Chips

Deep-frying has many of us (especially those of us of a certain age) still thinking, "Man, this can't be healthy." When you drop something in hot oil to be fried, the sizzling is caused by the food releasing its water content. The hot oil bath forces the steam out of the food being fried, forming a nice crispy exterior. It's estimated that the amount of oil absorbed in deep-frying might actually be less than pan-frying—the caveat being that if the oil is not hot enough, or if you cook something too long, your food could end up absorbing a lot more oil than intended. Whenever we make the choice to cook this way, we fry a bunch of different things. Sweet potato chips, yuca fries, even fried zucchini or summer squash (tossed in a light coating of tapioca or arrowroot flour) make for a great way to get veggies into the little ones. Oh, and if we are deep-frying, we almost always make some of our Chicken Nuggets Redux (page 47) and use the opportunity to deep-fry those, just like a certain fast-food chain. Serve plain, with Lime Mayonnaise (page 212), or sprinkled with a little cinnamon for a sweet and salty combination.

MAKES ABOUT 4 DOZEN CHIPS / PREP TIME: 5 MINUTES / TOTAL TIME: 20 MINUTES

2 cups fat (coconut oil, tallow, lard, or palm oil)

2 green plantains (slightly yellow for a sweeter chip), peeled and sliced into thin chips

½ teaspoon sea salt

1. Heat the oil in a large, deep Dutch oven or other heavy pan to 350° to 375°F. (To make sure the oil is hot enough, use a deep-fry thermometer. If you don't have one, drop a plantain into the oil. If it sizzles and drops beneath the surface then comes right up, the oil is ready; if it sinks and does not come up, the oil is not hot enough. If it sits on the surface, it may be too hot.)

2. Once at temperature, drop in some of the plantain slices (12 or so at a time). Use a large wire skimmer/strainer to flip over the pieces as needed, and cook until lightly browned and crisped, 1 to 2 minutes. Remove to a plate lined with paper towels and sprinkle with some of the salt while still hot. Repeat the process with the remaining slices.

Lemon Curd Bites

Light and lemony, this dessert has just enough sweetness to keep non-Paleo folks happy, and lots of nutty goodness thanks to the coconut. Topped with some fresh fruit, this is a perfect summertime treat.

SERVES 4 / PREP TIME: 5 MINUTES / TOTAL TIME: 5 MINUTES, PLUS AT LEAST 20 MINUTES CHILLING TIME

4 tablespoons (2 ounces) unsalted grass-fed butter

¼ cup coconut oil, melted

¼ cup full-fat coconut milk

2 tablespoons raw, local honey (see Note)

Grated zest of 1 lemon

½ cup fresh lemon juice (about 2 lemons)

2 teaspoons tapioca flour

3 tablespoons unsweetened shredded coconut, divided

1. In a small saucepan, melt the butter, coconut oil, and coconut milk. Bring to a simmer, then whisk in the honey and lemon zest.

2. In a separate bowl, whisk together the lemon juice with the tapioca flour. Slowly pour into the saucepan, whisking constantly. Remove from the heat and stir in all but 1 teaspoon of the shredded coconut.

3. Divide the lemon mixture among 4 small (4 ounces or less) cups or ramekins, and refrigerate for at least 20 minutes. Serve sprinkled with the reserved coconut.

NOTE: *If you prefer these a bit sweeter, add more honey or a little less lemon juice.*

Flourless Chocolate Mini Cakes

This is a decadent, almost pudding-like dessert that makes for a very special treat. Topped with some Whipped Coconut Cream (page 235) or heavy cream and served hot out of the oven, these are sure to satisfy your sweet tooth.

SERVES 8 / PREP TIME: 10 MINUTES / TOTAL TIME: 25 MINUTES

9 tablespoons (4.5 ounces) unsalted grass-fed butter, cut into chunks, plus more for greasing the ramekins

6 ounces fair trade dark chocolate (70% to 80% cacao), coarsely chopped (see Note)

3 large eggs, separated

2 tablespoons coconut sugar

A few drops peppermint extract or ⅛ teaspoon instant espresso powder (optional)

1. Preheat the oven to 350°F. Liberally grease 8 small (4-ounce) ramekins with butter.

2. Melt the chocolate and 9 tablespoons butter together in the microwave or in a double boiler.

3. In a medium bowl, whisk together the egg yolks and coconut sugar until pale yellow. Fold a little bit of the chocolate mixture into the egg yolks to temper them, then add the remaining chocolate mixture and stir well to combine.

4. In a clean bowl, beat the egg whites until stiff peaks form. Fold the beaten whites into the chocolate mixture. If desired, stir in the peppermint extract or espresso powder.

5. Spoon the batter into the ramekins and place the ramekins on a baking sheet. Bake until a toothpick inserted comes out with some crumbs clinging to it, about 12 minutes.

NOTE: *Some fair trade brands we like include Endangered Species, Alter Eco, Divine, Theo, and Green & Black's.*

ACKNOWLEDGMENTS

This book would not exist were it not for many events, many hours, but most of all—and most important—for the many people who have influenced its creation and our lives.

To all of you holding this book, thank you. Thank you for being a part of this journey, for wanting nothing but the best for yourself and your family, and for your faith in us that we can help you. We're going to do our best to do everything we can to support you!

To Mark "Grizz" Adams, your artistry always amazes us and makes us and our food look good. Your friendship and partnership on this cookbook journey is so appreciated, especially while juggling so much.

To our editors—Deb Brody, who saw us through two babies and two books and brought us on with the William Morrow/HarperCollins family, and to Cara Bedick and Kara Zauberman, who took over this project full force and made us feel right at home: Thank you for your confidence in and support of us, and your willingness to bring the marketplace access to recipes that have the potential to impact people's health in a huge way. We are so grateful to work with you. We'd be remiss in not thanking the copyeditors, designers, and marketing team, including Katherine Turro in marketing, Maria Silva in publicity, production editor Rachel Meyers, and interior designer Suet Chong.

To Sally, Lisa, and the Lisa Ekus Group: We're delighted to be a part of the TLEG family, and are proud to call you our "agency of record." Thank you for everything.

To our blog readers (there are a few, right?), Facebookers, Twitterers, Instagrammers, Pinteresters, etc., we love connecting with you all, hearing about your successes, and figuring out how to help you. Thank you for being part of this great big online world of ours!

To our fellow bloggers, authors, coaches, and others in the world out there making a difference: Thank you for inspiring us and being a part of this connected circle of ours. Thank you for helping to bring more health to the masses. We feel so grateful to be a part of such a supportive community. A special thanks (from Julie) to Diana Rodgers, Michelle Tam, and Emily Deans, aka the "moms-of-a-certain-age" club, for too many reasons to list. Your friendship and texts mean so much.

To Robb Wolf and Nicki Violetti: Your impact on our lives cannot be put into words. Thank you for all that you have done and continue to do to change lives—most certainly ours. We love, respect, and admire you more than you'll know. "Some friends aren't really friends—they're family." Thanks for being part of our family. We love you.

To our families, who have shaped us into who we are today, thank you. We do so much of what we do because of and for you, and we cannot thank you enough for the unconditional love and support you have given to us.

And finally, to our littlest family members, our Paleo kiddos Scott and Adelyn. Writing this book and trying to be good parents to you both challenged us on many levels, but it also brought more resolve to both of us in wanting to give you two the absolute best in life. You mean more to us than you'll ever know, and have us striving to do better in all that we do. We love you!

RESOURCES

FOR MORE INFORMATION AND RECIPES ON PALEO/PRIMAL/ ANCESTRAL HEALTH:

Againstallgrain.com

Balancedbites.com

Chriskresser.com

Marksdailyapple.com

Meljoulwan.com

Nomnompaleo.com

Paleomg.com

Robbwolf.com

Sustainabledish.com

Thepaleomom.com

Whole30.com and Whole9life.com

FOR MORE ON GENERAL HEALTH, FITNESS, WELLNESS, AND SUSTAINABILITY:

AnimalWelfareApproved.org

Dansplan.com

Defending Beef: The Case for Sustainable Meat Production, Nicolette Hahn Niman (Chelsea Green)

Docparsley.com

Drperlmutter.com

Eatwild.com

Ericcressey.com

Evatstrengthandconditioning.com

Gymlaird.com

PaleoFoundation.com

Polyfacefarms.com and all books by Joel Salatin

Robertsontrainingsystems.com

Savory.global

Seafoodwatch.org

SustainableAgriculture.net

Wheatbelly.com

ONLINE SOURCES FOR INGREDIENTS AND COOKING SUPPLIES:

Amazon.com—You can find almost any ingredient or cooking supply you need here.

Instacart.com—This delivery service can be a big help if you can't leave the house and you need groceries quickly. Check the site to see if you are in their service area.

ModPaleo.com—prepared Paleo meals

Petespaleo.com—prepared Paleo meals

Premadepaleo.com—prepared Paleo meals

ThriveMarket.com— great discounts on lots of Paleo pantry staples

TropicalTraditions.com—wonderful source for coconut-related items

USWellnessmeats.com—retailer of grass-fed, pasture-raised meats

WhiteOakPastures.com—A Savory Institute Hub and farm offering grass-fed, pasture-raised meats and poultry

UNIVERSAL CONVERSION CHART

OVEN TEMPERATURE EQUIVALENTS

250°F = 120°C   350°F = 180°C   450°F = 230°C

275°F = 135°C   375°F = 190°C   475°F = 240°C

300°F = 150°C   400°F = 200°C   500°F = 260°C

325°F = 160°C   425°F = 220°C

MEASUREMENT EQUIVALENTS

Measurements should always be level unless directed otherwise.

⅛ teaspoon = 0.5 mL

¼ teaspoon = 1 mL

½ teaspoon = 2 mL

1 teaspoon = 5 mL

1 tablespoon = 3 teaspoons = ½ fluid ounce = 15 mL

2 tablespoons = ⅛ cup = 1 fluid ounce = 30 mL

4 tablespoons = ¼ cup = 2 fluid ounces = 60 mL

5⅓ tablespoons = ⅓ cup = 3 fluid ounces = 80 mL

8 tablespoons = ½ cup = 4 fluid ounces = 120 mL

10⅔ tablespoons = ⅔ cup = 5 fluid ounces = 160 mL

12 tablespoons = ¾ cup = 6 fluid ounces = 180 mL

16 tablespoons = 1 cup = 8 fluid ounces = 240 mL

INDEX

Note: Page references in *italics* indicate photographs.

A

Alcohol, in Paleo diet, 5–6
Almond flour, for recipes, 20
Anchovy(ies)
    Caesar-ish Dressing, 180
    -Garlic Sauce, *156*, 159
Apple(s)
    Celery Root and Cauliflower Soup, *34*, 35
    Crisps, 234
    and Fennel, Roast Pork Tenderloin with, *44*, 45
    Morning Glory Muffins Revisited, *232*, 233
    Spiced Pork Skillet, 204, *205*
    Turkey Cutlets with Stuffing, 132, *133*
    Warm Curry Chicken Salad, 166, *167*
Artichoke-Spinach Dip, Pan-Seared Frozen Steaks with, *196*, 197–98
Arugula
    Chicken with Peaches, Basil, and Tomatoes, *176*, 177
    Crispy Chicken with Peppery Pesto Pasta, 118–19, *119*
Asparagus and Salmon, One-Pan Roast, 116
Avocado(s)
    Caesar-ish Dressing, 180
    Chop Chop Salad, 180, *181*
    Eggs Colorado, 199
    Salad, 98
    Sauce, 215
    Soup with Scallops, 146, *147*

B

Bacon
    All-American Burgers, *40*, 41
    Broccoli Salad, 92, *93*
    and Cheddar Cauliflower, Mashed, 99
    Chicken, and Brussels Sprouts Skewers, *168*, 169
    Chop Chop Salad, 180, *181*
    Meat Mix #1: Italian, 52, *53*
    Pancetta-Wrapped Cod, 200, 201
    Pecan Sweet Potatoes, Mashed, *96*, 97
    Spaghetti Squash Fritters, *100*, 101
Baharat Seasoning, 221
Barbecue Bake, 136
Barbecue Sauce, No-Cook, 216, *217*
Barbecue Shrimp Stew, 174, *175*
Basil
    -Ginger Pork, 138, *139*
    Peaches, and Tomatoes, Chicken with, *176*, 177
    Sauce, 158
    Sauce and Tomatoes, Trout in Parchment with, 153
    and Sun-Dried Tomato Cauliflower, Mashed, 99
    Turkey or Chicken Pesto Pasta Bake, *134*, 135–36
BBQ Meatloaf Roll, 32, *33*
Beef
    All-American Burgers, *40*, 41
    BBQ Meatloaf Roll, 32, *33*
    buying, for recipes, 20
    Chile Colorado, 74–75, *75*
    Cube Steak with Mushrooms, *178*, 179
    Filet with Yuca Hash Browns, *50*, 51
    Kitchen Sink Stew, 76, *77*
    Meat Mix #1: Italian, 52, *53*
    Meat Mix #3: Southwestern, 55
    Meat Mix #4: Veggie, 56
    One-Pan Fajitas, 120, *121*
    Oven-Roasted Steaks with Broccoli and Cauliflower, *126*, 127
    Pan-Seared Frozen Steaks with Spinach-Artichoke Dip, *196*, 197–98
    Philly-Style Steak with Onions and Mushrooms, 202, *203*
    Skillet Steaks with Veggies and Potatoes, 130, *131*
    Sloppy Joes, 194, *195*

Beef (continued)

Slow Cooker Short Ribs, *84*, 85

Tomato Meat Bake, 136

Veggie Steak Salad with Asian Dressing, 184–85

Beurre Blanc, *156*, 160

Blackberry Sauce, Salmon with, 170, *171*

Broccoli

and Cauliflower, Oven-Roasted Steaks with, *126*, 127

Salad, 92, *93*

Brussels Sprout(s)

Chicken, and Bacon Skewers, *168*, 169

Roast Chicken Thighs with Veggies, 124, *125*

Buffalo Chicken Salad, *164*, 165

Burgers

All-American, *40*, 41

Fish, with Wasabi, 190, *191*

C

Cabbage

Chinois Chicken Salad, 150, *151*

Lime Chipotle Slaw, 94, *95*

Veggie Steak Salad with Asian Dressing, 184–85

Caesar-ish Dressing, 180

Cajun Spice Mix, 225

Cakes

Flourless Chocolate Mini, 244, *245*

Pumpkin Pie-Cakes, 236, *237*

Carnitas, *72*, 73

Carrot(s)

Cucumber and Seafood Salad, 189

Kitchen Sink Stew, 76, *77*

Lime Chipotle Slaw, 94, *95*

Pork Con Thuyen, *82*, 83

Roast Chicken Thighs with Veggies, 124, *125*

Root Veggie Hash, 106

Salad, *90*, 91

Cashews

Magic Nut Butter, 228, *229*

Roasty Toasty Pepper Dip, 220, *220*

Cast-iron skillets, cooking in, 103

Cauliflower. *See also* Cauliflower Rice

and Broccoli, Oven-Roasted Steaks with, *126*, 127

and Celery Root Soup, *34*, 35

Mashed (with Variations), 99

Cauliflower Rice, 30

Basil-Ginger Pork, 138, *139*

Cauliflower Egg Muffins, 107

Chicken Mushroom Rice Casserole, 42, *43*

Kung Pao Chicken, 62–63, *63*

Lamb and Rice Stew, *122*, 123

Shrimp and Grits II, 38–39, *39*

Spanish "Rice," 104, *105*

Spicy Sausage Gumbo, 28, *29*

Celery Root and Cauliflower Soup, *34*, 35

Cheese

Mashed Cheddar and Bacon Cauliflower, 99

in Paleo diet, 5

Chicken

Brussels Sprouts, and Bacon Skewers, *168*, 169

buying, for recipes, 20

Cacciatore, *110*, 111

Chop Chop Salad, 180, *181*

Crispy, with Peppery Pesto Pasta, 118–19, *119*

Ginger-Garlic, with Cilantro Sauce, 60, *61*

Green Enchiladas, 36, *37*

Kung Pao, 62–63, *63*

Mushroom Rice Casserole, 42, *43*

Nuggets Redux, *46*, 47–48

One-Pan Fajitas, 120, *121*

or Turkey Pesto Pasta Bake, 134, *135*–36

with Peaches, Basil, and Tomatoes, *176*, 177

Poached, Basic, 31

Roast, Basic, 26, *27*

Salad, Buffalo, *164*, 165

Salad, Chinois, 150, *151*

Salad, Traditional, *161*, 162

Salad, Walnut, *161*, 163

Salad, Warm Curry, 166, *167*

Stock, *208*, 209

Thighs, Roast, with Veggies, 124, *125*

Verde, 86–87, *87*

Chiles

Chile Colorado, 74–75, *75*

Chipotle Sauce, *226*, 227

Green Enchiladas, 36, *37*

Kung Pao Chicken, 62–63, *63*

Lime Chipotle Slaw, 94, *95*

Mashed Chipotle Lime Sweet Potatoes, *96*, 97

Pico de Gallo (Salsa Fresca), 218

Pork Chops with Butternut Squash Noodles and Guajillo Sauce, *64*, 65–66

Salsa Verde, 219

Southwestern Mashed Cauliflower, 99

Spicy Lamb Stir-Fry with Mint and Eggplant, 188

Chili

Chile Colorado, 74–75, *75*

Eggs Colorado, 199
Chili Powder, 225
Chinois Chicken Salad, 150, *151*
Chocolate
    buying, for recipes, 20
    Mini Cakes, Flourless, 244, *245*
    Toasted Bark, 238, *239*
Cilantro
    Pork Con Thuyen, *82*, 83
    Sauce, Ginger-Garlic Chicken with, 60, *61*
Clams, Angry, *144*, 145
Coconut
    Apple Crisps, 234
    Lemon Curd Bites, *242*, 243
Coconut milk
    buying, for recipes, 20
    Whipped Coconut Cream, 235
Coconut oil, for recipes, 20
Cod, Pancetta-Wrapped, *200*, 201
Crab(meat)
    Cucumber and Seafood Salad, 189
    Cucumber Salad and Beurre Blanc, Macadamia-
        Crusted Halibut with, 155
    Mango, and Jicama Salad, *182*, 183
    Seafood Sunrises, 143
Crisps, Apple, 234
Cucumber(s)
    Crabmeat Salad and Beurre Blanc, Macadamia-
        Crusted Halibut with, 155
    and Seafood Salad, 189
    Summer Roll in a Bowl, *172*, 173
    Veggie Steak Salad with Asian Dressing, 184–85
Currants
    Morning Glory Muffins Revisited, *232*, 233
    Warm Curry Chicken Salad, 166, *167*
Curry Chicken Salad, Warm, 166, *167*

D
Daikon
    Cucumber and Seafood Salad, 189
    Veggie Steak Salad with Asian Dressing, 184–85
Dairy, for recipes, 20
Desserts
    Apple Crisps, 234
    Flourless Chocolate Mini Cakes, 244, *245*
    Lemon Curd Bites, *242*, 243
    Pumpkin Pie-Cakes, 236, *237*
    Toasted Bark, 238, *239*

Dips
    Pepper, Roasty Toasty, 220, *220*
    Spinach-Artichoke, Pan-Seared Frozen Steaks with,
        196, 197–98
Dressing, Caesar-ish, 180

E
Eggplant and Mint, Spicy Lamb Stir-Fry with, 188
Egg(s)
    Cauliflower Muffins, 107
    Colorado, 199
    Seafood Sunrises, 143
Enchiladas, Green, 36, *37*

F
Fajitas, One-Pan, 120, *121*
Fajita Seasoning, 224
Fennel and Apples, Roast Pork Tenderloin with, *44*, 45
Fish. *See also* Anchovy(ies)
    Burgers with Wasabi, 190, *191*
    Cakes, Thai, *148*, 149
    cooking guidelines, 152
    Crispy-Skinned Pan-Seared Salmon Fillets with
        Spicy Tomato Sauce, 154
    Macadamia-Crusted Halibut with Beurre Blanc
        and Cucumber Crabmeat Salad, 155
    Olive-Crusted Flounder, *192*, 193
    One-Pan Roast Salmon and Asparagus, 116
    Pancetta-Wrapped Cod, *200*, 201
    preparing for cooking, 22
    Salmon with Blackberry Sauce, 170, *171*
    sauces for, *156*, 157–60
    Trout in Parchment with Tomatoes and Basil
        Sauce, 153
Flounder, Olive-Crusted, *192*, 193
Flours, substituting, note about, 23
Food sourcing and sustainability, 14–18
Fritters, Spaghetti Squash, *100*, 101
Fruits. *See also specific fruits*
    seasonal, list of, 19

G
Garlic
    -Anchovy Sauce, *156*, 159
    -Ginger Chicken with Cilantro Sauce, 60, *61*
    -Rosemary Mayonnaise, 213
Ginger
    -Basil Pork, 138, *139*

Ginger *(continued)*
  -Garlic Chicken with Cilantro Sauce, 60, *61*
  Tomato Sauce, Spicy, *156*, 158
Grains, in Paleo diet, 4
Green Beans and Mushrooms, Turkey with, 128, *129*
Greens. *See also* Arugula; Lettuce; Spinach
  Green Enchiladas, 36, *37*
Gumbo, Spicy Sausage, 28, *29*

H
Halibut, Macadamia-Crusted, with Beurre Blanc and
  Cucumber Crabmeat Salad, 155
Hash, Root Veggie, 106
Honey-Mustard Sauce, *49*, 212

J
Jicama, Crab, and Mango Salad, *182*, 183

K
Kung Pao Chicken, 62–63, *63*

L
Lamb
  and Rice Stew, *122*, 123
  Stir-Fry, Spicy, with Mint and Eggplant, 188
Leeks, cleaning, 22
Legumes, in Paleo diet, 4–5
Lemon Curd Bites, *242*, 243
Lettuce
  Basil-Ginger Pork, 138, *139*
  Chop Chop Salad, 180, *181*
  Philly-Style Steak with Onions and Mushrooms,
    202, *203*
  Pork Con Thuyen, *82*, 83
  Summer Roll in a Bowl, *172*, 173
Lime
  Chipotle Slaw, 94, *95*
  Mayonnaise, 212

M
Macadamia(s)
  -Crusted Halibut with Beurre Blanc and Cucumber
    Crabmeat Salad, 155
  Dukkah, 224
  Magic Nut Butter, 228, *229*
Mango
  Crab, and Jicama Salad, *182*, 183
  Summer Roll in a Bowl, *172*, 173
  Veggie Steak Salad with Asian Dressing,
    184–85

Mayonnaise
  Basic (with Variations), *210*, 211
  Wasabi, *156*, 157
Meal planning, 8–14
Meat. *See also* Beef; Pork; Venison
  Mix #1: Italian, 52, *53*
  Mix #2: Asian, 54
  Mix #3: Southwestern, 55
  Mix #4: Veggie, 56
  mixes, forming into meatballs, 57
  mixes, forming into meatloaves, 57
  preparing for cooking, 22
  Stuffed Zucchini Appetizer, 57
  and Sweet Potato Skillet, 112, *113*
Meatballs
  forming and cooking, 57
  Wonton-ish Soup, 58, *59*
Meatloaf Roll, BBQ, 32, *33*
Meatloaves, forming and cooking, 57
Morning Glory Muffins Revisited, *232*, 233
Moroccan Spice Blend, 222
Muffins
  Cauliflower Egg, 107
  Morning Glory, Revisited, *232*, 233
Mushroom(s)
  Chicken Cacciatore, *110*, 111
  Chicken Rice Casserole, 42, *43*
  cleaning, 21
  Crispy Prosciutto Salad, 186, *187*
  Cube Steak with, *178*, 179
  and Green Beans, Turkey with, 128, *129*
  Kitchen Sink Stew, 76, *77*
  and Onions, Philly-Style Steak with, 202, *203*
  Pork Medallions with Balsamic Mustard, 117
  Turkey Cutlets with Stuffing, 132, *133*
Mustard-Honey Sauce, *49*, 212

N
Nut(s)
  Butter, Magic, 228, *229*
  Dukkah, 224
  Mashed Bacon Pecan Sweet Potatoes, *96*, 97
  Roasty Toasty Pepper Dip, 220, *220*
  Toasted Bark, 238, *239*
  Walnut Chicken Salad, *161*, 163

O
Okra
  Barbecue Shrimp Stew, 174, *175*

and Shrimp Skillet, 137
  Spicy Sausage Gumbo, 28, *29*
Olive(s)
  Avocado Salad, 98
  Chicken Cacciatore, *110*, 111
  -Crusted Flounder, *192*, 193
  Salsa, *156*, 159
Onions and Mushrooms, Philly-Style Steak with, 202, *203*

P
Paleo
  for busy, budget-conscious families, 7–8
  definitions of, 1–3
  foods included in, 4–6
  meal planning, 8–14
  transitioning to, 6–7
Pancetta-Wrapped Cod, *200*, 201
Peaches, Basil, and Tomatoes, Chicken with, *176*, 177
Pecan(s)
  Bacon Sweet Potatoes, Mashed, *96*, 97
  Magic Nut Butter, 228, *229*
  Toasted Bark, *238, 239*
Pepper(s). *See also* Chiles
  Barbecue Shrimp Stew, 174, *175*
  Chicken Cacciatore, *110*, 111
  Chicken Verde, 86–87, *87*
  Dip, Roasty Toasty, 220, *220*
  Kung Pao Chicken, 62–63, *63*
  One-Pan Fajitas, 120, *121*
  Shrimp and Grits II, 38–39, *39*
  Skillet Steaks with Veggies and Potatoes, 130, *131*
  Spanish "Rice," 104, *105*
  Veggie Steak Salad with Asian Dressing, 184–85
Pesto Pasta, Peppery, Crispy Chicken with, 118–19, *119*
Pesto Pasta Bake, Turkey or Chicken, *134*, 135–36
Pico de Gallo (Salsa Fresca), 218
Pie-Cakes, Pumpkin, 236, *237*
Plantain Chips, 240, *241*
Pork. *See also* Bacon; Sausage(s)
  All-American Burgers, *40*, 41
  Barbecue Bake, 136
  Basil-Ginger, 138, *139*
  buying, for recipes, 20
  Carnitas, *72*, 73
  Chile Colorado, 74–75, *75*
  Chops with Butternut Squash Noodles and Guajillo Sauce, *64*, 65–66
  Con Thuyen, *82*, 83

Crispy Prosciutto Salad, 186, *187*
  Meat Mix #2: Asian, 54
  Medallions with Balsamic Mustard, 117
  Mole, 78, *79*
  Skillet, Spiced, 204, *205*
  Tenderloin, Roast, with Apples and Fennel, *44*, 45
  Tinga, 80–81, *81*
  Wonton-ish Soup, 58, *59*
Potatoes. *See also* Sweet Potato(es)
  Kitchen Sink Stew, 76, *77*
  and Veggies, Skillet Steaks with, 130, *131*
Poultry. *See also* Chicken; Turkey
  preparing for cooking, 22
Processed foods, in Paleo diet, 5–6
Prosciutto, Crispy, Salad, 186, *187*
Pumpkin Pie-Cakes, 236, *237*

R
Radishes
  Cucumber and Seafood Salad, 189
  Pork Con Thuyen, *82*, 83
  Veggie Steak Salad with Asian Dressing, 184–85
Raisins
  Broccoli Salad, *92*, 93
  Walnut Chicken Salad, *161*, 163
Recipes
  cooking times, 21
  ingredients for, 20
  measuring ingredients for, 22
  seasoning for, 21
  serving sizes, 23
  substituting ingredients, 23
  washing fish, meat, and poultry for, 22
  washing produce for, 21–22
Rosemary-Garlic Mayonnaise, 213

S
Salads
  Avocado, 98
  Broccoli, *92*, 93
  Carrot, *90*, 91
  Chicken, Buffalo, *164*, 165
  Chicken, Chinois, 150, *151*
  Chicken, Traditional, *161*, 162
  Chicken, Walnut, *161*, 163
  Chicken, Warm Curry, 166, *167*
  Chop Chop, 180, *181*
  Crab, Mango, and Jicama, *182*, 183
  Crispy Prosciutto, 186, *187*

Salads (*continued*)
Cucumber and Seafood, 189
Lime Chipotle Slaw, 94, *95*
Veggie Steak, with Asian Dressing, 184–85
Salmon
and Asparagus, One-Pan Roast, 116
with Blackberry Sauce, 170, *171*
Fillets, Crispy-Skinned Pan-Seared, with Spicy
Tomato Sauce, 154
Fish Burgers with Wasabi, 190, *191*
Salsa
Fresca (Pico de Gallo), 218
Olive, *156*, 159
Verde, 219
Salt, for recipes, 20
Sauces. *See also* Salsa
Anchovy-Garlic, *156*, 159
Asian Dipping, 54
Avocado, 215
Basic Mayonnaise (with Variations),
210, 211
Basil, 158
Beurre Blanc, *156*, 160
Chipotle, *226*, *227*
for fish, *156*, 157–60
Ginger Tomato, Spicy, *156*, 158
Honey-Mustard, *49*, 212
Magic Nut Butter, 228, *229*
No-Cook Barbecue, 216, *217*
Olive Salsa, *156*, 159
Tomato, 5-Ingredient, 214
Wasabi Mayonnaise, *156*, 157
Sausage(s)
Angry Clams, *144*, 145
BBQ Meatloaf Roll, 32, *33*
Gumbo, Spicy, 28, *29*
Homemade Chorizo, 68, *69*
Pork Tinga, 80–81, *81*
Tomato Meat Bake, 136
Scallops, Avocado Soup with, 146, *147*
Seeds
Dukkah, 224
Shellfish. *See also* Shrimp
Angry Clams, *144*, 145
Avocado Soup with Scallops, 146, *147*
Crab, Mango, and Jicama Salad, *182*, *183*
Cucumber and Seafood Salad, 189
Macadamia-Crusted Halibut with Beurre Blanc
and Cucumber Crabmeat Salad, 155
Seafood Sunrises, 143

Shrimp
Creamy, with Vegetables, *114*, 115
Cucumber and Seafood Salad, 189
and Grits II, 38–39, *39*
and Okra Skillet, 137
Seafood Sunrises, 143
Spicy Sriracha Bake, 136
Stew, Barbecue, 174, *175*
Summer Roll in a Bowl, *172*, 173
Slaw, Lime Chipotle, 94, *95*
Sloppy Joes, 194, *195*
Soups
Avocado, with Scallops, 146, *147*
Celery Root and Cauliflower, *34*, 35
Wonton-ish, 58, *59*
Spanish "Rice," 104, *105*
Spice Blends
Baharat Seasoning, 221
Cajun Spice Mix, 225
Chili Powder, 225
Dukkah, 224
Fajita Seasoning, 224
Moroccan, 222
Steak Seasoning, 223
Spinach
-Artichoke Dip, Pan-Seared Frozen Steaks with,
196, 197–98
BBQ Meatloaf Roll, 32, *33*
Creamy Shrimp with Vegetables, *114*, 115
Crispy Prosciutto Salad, 186, *187*
Squash. *See also* Zucchini
Butternut, Noodles and Guajillo Sauce, Pork
Chops with, 64, 65–66
Pork Medallions with Balsamic Mustard, 117
Pumpkin Pie-Cakes, 236, *237*
Skillet Steaks with Veggies and Potatoes, 130, *131*
Spaghetti, Fritters, 100, 101
spaghetti, how to cook, 102
Turkey or Chicken Pesto Pasta Bake, *134*, 135–36
Sriracha
Bake, Spicy, 136
-Sesame Mayonnaise, 212
Steak Seasoning, 223
Stews
Barbecue Shrimp, 174, *175*
Kitchen Sink, 76, *77*
Lamb and Rice, *122*, 123
Pork Mole, 78, *79*
Spicy Sausage Gumbo, 28, *29*

Stock, Chicken, *208, 209*
Sugar, in Paleo diet, 5–6
Summer Roll in a Bowl, *172, 173*
Sustainability and food sourcing, 14–18
Sweet Potato(es)
    Buffalo Chicken Salad, *164,* 165
    Mashed (with Variations), *96,* 97
    and Meat Skillet, 112, *113*
    Pork Mole, 78, *79*
    Pork Tinga, 80–81, *81*
    Roast Chicken Thighs with Veggies, 124, *125*
    Root Veggie Hash, 106

T

Thai Fish Cakes, *148,* 149
Tomatillos
    Salsa Verde, 219
Tomato(es)
    Avocado Salad, 98
    and Basil Sauce, Trout in Parchment with, 153
    Chicken Cacciatore, *110,* 111
    Chop Chop Salad, 180, *181*
    Crispy Prosciutto Salad, 186, *187*
    Eggs Colorado, 199
    Ginger Sauce, Spicy, *156,* 158
    Meat Bake, 136
    No-Cook Barbecue Sauce, 216, *217*
    Olive Salsa, *156,* 159
    Peaches, and Basil, Chicken with, *176,* 177
    Pico de Gallo (Salsa Fresca), 218
    Pork Tinga, 80–81, *81*
    Sauce, 5-Ingredient, 214
    Sauce, Spicy, Crispy-Skinned Pan-Seared Salmon
        Fillets with, 154
    Sloppy Joes, 194, *195*
    Spanish "Rice," 104, *105*
    Spicy Sausage Gumbo, 28, *29*
    Sun-Dried, and Basil Cauliflower, Mashed, 99
    Vegetable Marinara Bake, 136
Trout in Parchment with Tomatoes and Basil Sauce, 153
Tuna
    Fish Burgers with Wasabi, 190, *191*
    Thai Fish Cakes, *148, 149*

Turkey
    Cutlets with Stuffing, 132, *133*
    with Mushrooms and Green Beans, 128, *129*
    or Chicken Pesto Pasta Bake, *134,* 135–36

V

Vegetable(s)
    leafy green, washing, 22
    Marinara Bake, 136
    Meat Mix #4: Veggie, 56
    noodles, how to make, 67
    Roast Chicken Thighs with Veggies, 124, *125*
    Root Veggie Hash, 106
    seasonal, list of, 19
    Veggie Steak Salad with Asian Dressing,
        184–85
Venison
    Cube Steak with Mushrooms, *178,* 179
    Meat Mix #3: Southwestern, 55
    Meat Mix #4: Veggie, 56

W

Walnut Chicken Salad, *161,* 163
Wasabi
    Fish Burgers with, 190, *191*
    Mayonnaise, *156,* 157
Whipped Coconut Cream, 235
Wonton-ish Soup, 58, *59*

Y

Yuca Hash Browns, Beef Filet with,
    50, 51

Z

Zucchini
    Creamy Shrimp with Vegetables, *114,* 115
    Crispy Chicken with Peppery Pesto Pasta, 118–19,
        119
    Ginger-Garlic Chicken with Cilantro Sauce, 60, *61*
    Morning Glory Muffins Revisited, *232,* 233
    Skillet Steaks with Veggies and Potatoes,
        130, *131*
    Stuffed, Appetizer, 57

BOOKS BY
JULIE & CHARLES MAYFIELD

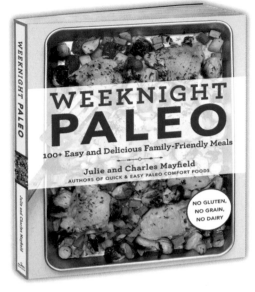

WEEKNIGHT PALEO
100+ Easy and Delicious Family-Friendly Meals
Available in Paperback and E-book

The bestselling authors are back with easy, delicious, family-friendly Paleo recipes for dinner, featuring plenty of proteins, fruits, vegetables, and healthy fats.

Here are 100+ satisfying Paleo recipes to add variety and keep your family well fed, no matter how hectic or busy your day. For those new to Paleo or in need of a refresher, the Mayfields provide prep tips and meal plans to organize weekly meals.

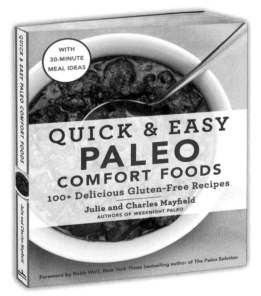

QUICK & EASY PALEO COMFORT FOODS
100+ Delicious Gluten-Free Recipes
Available in Paperback and E-book

The wildly popular Paleo movement is going strong, with millions of people enjoying the healthy, fat-trimming benefits that come with eliminating gluten, legumes, and dairy from their diets. In this gorgeous cookbook, Paleo pioneers Julie and Charles Mayfield have gathered an impressive selection of palate-pleasing, timesaving Paleo recipes that are not only nutritious and delicious, but quick and easy to prepare.

Packed with delicious ideas for starters and snacks, soups, stews, and salads, main dishes, sauces and sides, and sweets and treats, *Quick & Easy Paleo Comfort Foods* includes tips and recipes to help you transform favorite dishes and go-to comfort foods into healthy, gluten-free meals every day.